Historical Scholarship in the United States

and Other Essays

HISTORICAL

SCHOLARSHIP

IN THE

UNITED STATES

AND OTHER ESSAYS

By W. Stull Holt

UNIVERSITY OF WASHINGTON PRESS

SEATTLE AND LONDON

d

Copyright © 1967 by the University of Washington Press
Library of Congress Catalog Card Number 67-13114
Printed in the United States of America

Acknowledgments

PART I. "Historians During the Late Nineteenth Century" was originally published as the Introduction to *Historical Scholarship in the United States, 1876-1901: As Revealed in the Correspondence of Herbert B. Adams* (Baltimore, Md.: The Johns Hopkins Press, 1938). "The Idea of Scientific History in America" first appeared in *Journal of the History of Ideas,* I (June, 1940), 352-362. "Historical Scholarship in the Twentieth Century" was originally published as "Historical Scholarship," in *American Scholarship in the Twentieth Century,* ed. Merle Curti (Cambridge, Mass.: Harvard Univerity Press, 1953), pp. 83-110. "Who Reads the Best Histories?" appeared in the *Mississippi Valley Historical Review,* XL (March, 1954), 613-619. "History and the Social Sciences Reconsidered" originally appeared in *Kyklos,* Fasc. 4 (1955), pp. 389-396. It is a review of *The Social Sciences in Historical Study: A Report of the Committee on Historiography* (New York: Social Science Research Council, Bulletin No. 64, 1954). "An Evaluation of the Report on Theory and Practice in Historical Study" was first published in the

Pacific Historical Review, XVIII (May, 1949), 233-242. "The Education of Historians in the United States" is from the *American Historical Review,* LXVIII (January, 1963), 402-406. PART II. "The United States and the Defense of the Western Hemisphere, 1815-1940" was originally published in *Pacific Historical Review,* X (March, 1941), 29-38. "Uncle Sam as Deer, Jackal, and Lion OR The United States in Power Politics" appeared first in *Pacific Spectator,* III (Winter, 1949), 41-54. "What Wilson Sent and What House Received: Or Scholars Need to Check Carefully" was first published in the *American Historical Review,* LXV (April, 1960), 569-571. "American Security and Historical and Geographical Accidents," previously unpublished, was presented as a lecture to history students at the University of Oregon in March, 1961. PART III. "Some Consequences of the Urban Movement in American History" was W. Stull Holt's presidential address at the 1952 meeting of the Pacific Coast Branch of the American Historical Association. It was published in the *Pacific Historical Review,* XXII (November, 1953), 337-351.

Contents

PART III: THE URBAN MOVEMENT IN AMERICAN HISTORY

Introduction

In June, 1967, on the forty-first anniversary of his taking the doctorate, W. Stull Holt retires as professor of history at the University of Washington. This volume, containing many of his hitherto scattered essays, is published as a tribute to him as teacher, scholar, colleague, and devoted friend. If these essays now succeed in reaching a new audience of readers who will be provoked by their many suggestive insights, and if scholars embark on fresh lines of historical investigation indicated by these essays, the tribute will be enhanced mightily.

Professor Holt has never been a narrow specialist. His interests as teacher and scholar have spanned the totality of the American past. It was the First World War, through which he lived as student and as military flier on the Western Front, that exercised a profound influence on his future career. He emerged from the war a confirmed Wilsonian but without the conviction of the moral idealist. In his view, President Wilson's great accomplishment in foreign affairs was his leadership in the movement for collective security and a realistic awareness of the changed conditions in international existence which affected the United States. For Professor Holt, America's tragic mistake was in not accepting the responsibilities commensurate with its vast power in the world during the 1920's and the 1930's. Perhaps because of these views, he chose as the subject for his dissertation at The Johns Hopkins University the tracing of the historical experience of the United States Senate in rejecting treaties submitted for its consideration and ratification by American Chief Executives. Although Professor Holt's interest in the processes of formulation and execution of American foreign policy has been active and continuous, he also saw other historical processes of importance to his generation, and to these he likewise turned his attention.

During the 1920's, Professor Holt prepared under the auspices of the Brookings Institution a series of monographs surveying the history of various administrative bureaus of the federal government. It was apparent that the bureaucracy was growing rapidly, but historians had hardly acknowledged the tendency toward "big government" and monstrous public administration. His work was certainly not intended to be more than introductory, but it did indicate what might be expected from systematic research in this direction. In much the same way that he was attracted to administrative history, Professor Holt was attracted to the history of urbanization. He regarded the aggregations of population in large metropolitan centers and the attendant mobility of the American population, particularly the movement from rural to urban, as possibly the central fact of modern American development. Although he published but few articles himself, he encouraged his students —both at the John Hopkins University during the 1930's and later at the University of Washington—to pursue research in this field, and several valuable publications resulted.

Notwithstanding these diverse interests, Professor Holt was at all times keenly interested in the study of historiography and how historians acting individually or collectively went about the task of writing history. Never one to avoid controversies, he became deeply involved in the debates between orthodox and revisionist interpreters concerning the origins of the First and Second World Wars. He engaged in the arguments spurred by the publications of the several Social Science Research Council Bulletins that considered the current status of historical studies during the 1940's and the 1950's. Being an historian with eclectic interests and a bent toward engaging in intellectual dialogue between the mid-1920's and the mid-1960's did not allow for lucrative employment; the many controversies, however, offered the prime ingredients for a lively professional existence.

Professor Holt's classes, particularly the graduate seminars, reflected this heightened sense of excitement. History was never a monotonous sequence of events. The historian undertook an enormous and weighty responsibility. He was at once a detective who searched for the evidence. Later, as prosecutor, his was the job of presenting the case; as defense counsel he had to conduct a constant cross-examination while at the same time maintaining a sympathetic view of his client's interests. Then, in the capacity of judge, it was incumbent on the historian to pronounce some verdict on the evidence. Throughout, the historian was obligated to write honestly and clearly without any a priori interpretation. Because he was required to play all the roles in the courtroom of posterity, he must never indulge in writing a trial brief. Here then were many challenges that historical scholarship offered its practitioners. Those students who participated in Professor Holt's seminars often realized that they were not only learning about history and historical method, they were in the presence of a masterful critic who was working at what he loved best to do.

It would indeed be misleading to think of Professor Holt as having an exclusive commitment to the classroom. In his scheme of values, the historian in order to be an effective scholar and teacher must become involved in the life of his institution, his community, and the large world outside. Acting on this premise, Professor Holt assumed an active participation in important university committees. He served as a frequent consultant to candidates aspiring for elective office. During the Second World War, he volunteered for military service with the United States Air Force. During 1963-64, he agreed to serve as Managing Editor of the *American Historical Review* and as Executive Secretary of the American Historical Association. These extracurricular forays were in keeping with Professor Holt's basic view that the academic historian should not insulate himself from his contemporaries. Now that he is retiring from active classroom instruction, no one who knows Stull Holt really expects him to retire from the many intellectual and political interests which he has cultivated so well.

LAWRENCE E. GELFAND
ROBERT A. SKOTHEIM

December, 1966

Part I

Historical Scholarship

and the Historical Profession

Historians During the Late Nineteenth Century

To the student of American historiography there is no period comparable in interest to the years between 1876 when Herbert B. Adams was appointed a fellow in the Johns Hopkins University and 1901 when he died. In part this is because of the presence of certain ideas which either as avowed philosophy or as unconscious prepossessions affected the history written. Prominent among these were that complex of ideas labelled Darwinism and the related belief that history is or should be a science. In part the period is so rich a one to study because of the achievements of the historians during it. Both in quantity and in quality the historical output was remarkable. Moreover, two distinct forms of historical writing, the broad canvas and the miniature, flourished side by side. It was the golden age of the Titans who scaled the historical heaven by piling volume on volume. It was also the period during which the monograph, born of the new specialization, became the characteristic form of scholarly history.

But what gives the last quarter of the nineteenth century

a unique interest is the fact that historical scholarship then became a profession. Only a bare handful of men had previously made a career of historical study and writing. In no sense of the word had the study of history been a profession. Historical scholarship and the writing of history had been the avocation of lawyers, clergy or businessmen.

When Herbert Adams began his career at the Johns Hopkins in 1876 almost no history had been written by American university professors. Indeed, there had been almost no professors of history to write any. Andrew D. White noted that before he accepted the professorship in history at Michigan in 1857, "there was not at that time a professor of history pure and simple in any American University."[1] The teaching of history in most universities had been left to men primarily interested in other subjects so that history received, as Charles Kendall Adams complained, "only such charitable attention as could be given it by some benevolent professor after his energies had already been too much exhausted by the absolute necessities of what was thought to be more important instruction."[2] By 1880 there were only eleven professors of history in the United States.[3]

Within one generation a revolution had been effected. Its results can be seen in the personnel of the two notable cooperative histories of the period. In the earlier one, Justin Winsor's *Narrative and Critical History of America,* two of

[1] Andrew D. White, *Autobiography of Andrew Dickson White* (New York, 1905), I, 255.

[2] Charles Kendall Adams, *A Manual of Historical Literature* (New York, 1888), p. 1. Some of the combinations seemed ludicrous after a generation of specialization. Thus Brander Matthews, as a student at Columbia in the seventies, found one professor teaching mental and moral philosophy, political economy, logic, English literature and history. "It was," Matthews observed, "not only a chair that he filled, or even a settee; it was a series of settees rising row on row." Brander Matthews, "College in the Seventies," *Columbia University Quarterly,* XIX, 134.

[3] *Historical Scholarship in America* (New York, 1932), p. 4. The statement is in the Introduction written by J. Franklin Jameson.

the thirty-four authors were professors of history and only eight others were university professors of other subjects. Of the entire number only one had received graduate training in history. In the American Nation Series, which appeared between 1904 and 1907, twenty-one of the twenty-four authors were university professors and all but two of them had done graduate work in history. That shift marked the trend of the times. When Herbert Adams died in 1901, no one could doubt that historical scholarship in America and the writing of history with any pretense to scholarly qualities were, for better or for worse, in the custody of university professors.[4]

Herbert B. Adams not only witnessed the process but played a larger part than any other one man in America in the establishment of the historical profession. Consequently his correspondence is a proper source for the study of various significant aspects of the movement.[5] Although it is expected that the letters here presented will speak for themselves, a little judicious prompting may help.

In the first place it is necessary to remember that these letters are distinctly written by one member of a profession to another. They are about courses being given, the number of students, textbooks, subjects being investigated, jobs and other similar professional matters. To people who consider such things trivial the letters will have no significance. To

[4] Curiously, although the fact is a commonplace, no one has yet studied the results to ascertain in what ways the history written under the new regime is better or worse or different. The most thoughtful discussion I have found is in the inaugural address of J. Franklin Jameson as professor of history in the University of Chicago. *University Record* (January, 1902), VI, 294-300.

[5] Adams kept no copies of the letters he wrote except in a few instances and then usually when discussing business rather than scholarly matters. The letters of his printed below constitute a fairly large proportion of those that have been found. Several are from the Andrew D. White Papers in the Cornell University library, and Dr. Frederic Bancroft generously permitted copies to be made of the letters Adams had written to him.

persons seeking the observations of intelligent men on contemporary events they will be intensely disappointing. The
several hundred letters written during the period of the Spanish American War and of the contest over the ratification
of the peace treaty contain only several passing references
to those exciting events. Although the writers were students
of history they were, if one judged by these letters alone,
so absorbed in their professional problems as to be oblivious
to life surrounding them. Such a judgment would probably
be incorrect. Herbert Adams certainly insisted that "Politics
is present history." It is more accurate to conclude that in
this correspondence they were writing not in the spirit of
Horace Walpole but as one chemist might describe test tubes,
laboratory technique and experiments to another.

For that very reason the letters will be of value to persons
interested in the historical profession—a value artificially
enhanced because there are practically no similar letters available in print. They cast some light, for instance, on the
spread of historical scholarship through the country. This
subject greatly interested Adams. He liked to refer to other
universities where his students had gone to introduce the
new scholarly methods as colonies. He had a map on the
wall in which he stuck pins wherever a former student was
teaching, and in numerous articles he dwelt with emphasis
on the various university positions held by Hopkins graduates.
Some letters are included to illustrate how university positions
were filled, the salaries paid, the stipulations made, the services expected—all of these factors being obviously important
to students of the profession.

Another subject on which the letters cast light is the contact between Adams and European scholars. The situation
revealed is one that surprised me greatly. I had assumed that
Adams, the graduate of a German university, the historian
of the Germanic origins of New England towns and the man

who is supposed to have introduced German seminar methods at the Johns Hopkins, would have held German scholarship in the greatest esteem and would have kept in the closest possible touch with many German scholars. Apparently the reverse is nearer the truth. Among the thousands of letters preserved there are only a scant dozen from Germany and most of them are of no consequence. It is also obvious from other letters that Adams neither wrote to his former German professors nor sent them his historical publications, and that his admiration for German scholarship was by no means unqualified. On the other hand the letters testify to a much more intimate contact with English scholars. The number and eminence of the Englishmen who visited the Johns Hopkins and with whom Adams corresponded suggests the possibility that the orthodox account of the dominant influence of German scholarship in America during this period may need revision.

Interesting as is the question of the European influences on the new scholarly profession, its American environment was of more concern, certainly to the men who wrote to Adams. Accordingly many of the letters contain references indicating the general intellectual atmosphere and the condition of education. Many were written by young men fired with professional zeal and in a hurry to succeed in their chosen career so that allowance must be made for complaints of discouraging conditions. Nevertheless, there is an explanation of much in the intellectual scene in Trent's description of his surroundings or in Bassett's wish that someone would present a picture of Lincoln so that he could make an address on that subject at Trinity College in North Carolina.

One of the first things that the members of a scholarly profession are apt to do is to form an organization for mutual encouragement, for the promotion of the interests of the group and for increasing the aids to research. So it was with the professional historians. Herbert Adams was the moving spirit both in the formation of the American Historical Association in 1884 and in the conduct of its affairs for many years afterwards. A number of the letters refer to its activities and career. It is possible to appreciate fully the fact that great history cannot be organized into being and yet recognize the many important ways in which the organization of scholarly work prevents wasted effort and raises the standards of the profession. The independent suggestions that a scholarly journal for the profession be started is evidence of how keenly the need for that particular piece of machinery was felt.

Enough has, perhaps, been said to indicate some of the reasons for which these letters were selected and some of the uses to which they may be put. They can, however, be more wisely interpreted if certain of the facts concerning the career of Herbert Adams and the work in history at the Johns Hopkins are borne in mind.[6]

The fellowship to which Adams was appointed in 1876 was something new in America, for post-doctoral grants to enable young scholars to engage in research had been unknown. Although no teaching duties were required of him, he had two classes in his first year. Both were entirely voluntary for students as well as teacher. One class of two students met once a week with European history as the subject. The other class with one student consisted of a walk and a talk on American constitutional history twice a week. In 1878 Adams was promoted to the rank of Associate and to a salary of $1,000. In the academic year 1878-1879 he taught

---

[6] The fullest sketch of Herbert B. Adams is that by John Martin Vincent in *American Masters of Social Science* (New York, 1927), edited by Howard W. Odum. A number of appreciation accounts of his career were published in 1902 as an extra volume of the Hopkins *Studies*. In this memorial volume is a bibliography of the published scholarly work of the faculty and students who had been in the department.

his first regular classes. They included a class in European History during the Middle Ages meeting four times a week during the first half year, a class in German History meeting twice a week for two months and a class in Political Economy meeting twice a week for two months. In addition to these courses he gave ten public lectures on the Beginnings of Church and State. During the second half of the year and similarly during the next several years Adams taught at Smith College. One other course claimed his presence. This was the seminar in history directed by Dr. Austin Scott, who once each week left his regular work in Washington as assistant to George Bancroft and took charge of the new seminar in Baltimore. Scott, with an appointment as Associate, had begun this work when the University opened in 1876 and continued in it until 1882.

Obviously the slight contact of Scott, the courses of the young Herbert Adams and the occasional series of lectures by visiting scholars did not constitute a program of graduate work in history that satisfied President Gilman. Between 1876 and 1881 a number of men then enjoying established reputations as historical scholars were invited to take charge of the work in history at the Hopkins. Professor J. L. Diman of Brown University had been offered a permanent position on the Hopkins faculty by Gilman in May, 1876, but replied that domestic circumstances prevented him from considering it. In December, 1877, Henry Adams was approached and at one time apparently consented to accept a temporary appointment. Nothing came of these conversations. In July, 1879 and again in the summer of 1880, Professor Hermann E. von Holst of Freiburg was offered a professorship in history. After protracted negotiations he refused. In November, 1880, T. M. Cooley, a judge and a professor of law at the University of Michigan, was offered a professorship in jurisprudence and with it was to go the responsibility of leadership in related subjects including history. He, too, declined the appointment.[7]

Gilman had warned Adams that the appointment of a senior professor might jeopardize his position, but whatever danger there might have been became remote after 1881. In the autumn of that year Adams for the first time was placed in charge of the Historical Seminary which he devoted to original investigations of what he called American Institutional History. The publication of the results of the research done by his students and by himself began in 1882 when the first numbers of *The Johns Hopkins University Studies in Historical and Political Science* appeared. This was the first such series in history in the United States and its appearance created something of a sensation. The new University had previously made possible the publication of several scholarly journals in other fields, and nothing Gilman and his associates did contributed more to the reputation of the Hopkins as a center of advanced scholarly work. The period had begun in the United States when the publication of research was the great desideratum among members of university faculties.

Adams had by this time won an assured place on the Hopkins faculty. In 1883, the year in which he was offered the professorship at the University of Pennsylvania to which McMaster was subsequently appointed, he was promoted to the rank of Associate Professor with a salary of $2,750. The program of studies he then considered best for a graduate student was described at length in the draft of a statement dated February 6, 1884. It reads:

---

[7] The correspondence relating to these offers is in the files of President Gilman in the archives of the Johns Hopkins University. A brief account of the negotiations with Henry Adams is in *The New England Quarterly* (September, 1938), XI, 632-638.

REQUIREMENTS AND DISCIPLINE
IN THE COURSE FOR PH.D. HISTORY AND POLITICAL SCIENCE

1. The candidate must pass all required examinations, some of which occur the first year of his graduate course, in (1) his principle [*sic*] subject which may be either History or Political Science and (2) in two subordinate subjects, both akin to his major course. For example, History may [be] associated as major with International Law and Political Economy as minors.

2. The Ph.D. course presupposes an acquaintance with general hist. & with polit. econ. equivalent in amount to that obtained in the undergraduate courses of this University & this matter will be tested.

3. The course absolutely requires a reading acquaintance with French and German authors representing the most advanced stage of Hist. & Polit. Sci. as seen in special lit. & the regular journals.

4. A thorough knowledge of some special field is requisite for a major course in Hist. or Political Science, which though limited shall nevertheless be sufficiently broad to illustrate general truth, the theory being that the way to the general is through that which is special or *universalia in rebus.* For example, when History is taken as the major subject, the student may specialize upon Institutional History (embracing Ancient Society, Classic & Modern European States); or, he may pursue the subject of Church History (including Church and State); or, again, the Const. Hist. of Eng. and of the U.S. When Political Science is taken as a major course, a very special knowledge of some one large subject is demanded, as Political Economy, including all its subdivisions (Theory, Hist. of Economics, Finance, Social Questions) or a Science of Gov. including Polit. Philos. Con. Politics & Administration. For minor course any two branches of a major subject akin to the major course actually taken may be offered, e.g. Polit. Philos. & Finance with Hist. or Classical Hist. & Engl. Hist. with Polit. Sci.

5. In all subjects, major or minor, an acquaintance with original sources of information for some limited period & upon some special topic will [be] exacted.

6. In all subjects an extension of private reading will be demanded, e.g. in Eng. & Amer. Hist. Elton, Allen, Guest, Stubbs, Hallam, May, Madison, Elliotts Debates, Bancroft, Von Holst, in Polit. Econ. as major.

7. Attendance upon all lectures class-exercises & sem. work required

of grad. students in Hist. & Polit. Sci. This attendance averages from
10-12 hours per week.

8. The lectures in Hist. & Pol. Sci. aim at the presentation of (a) the
best sources of information, primary & secondary, (b) representative &
suggestive topics, which shall not only convey pos. knowledge but open
up lines of special reading & original research.

9. Class-exercises for graduates comprise (a) oral reports & joint
discussions upon appointed themes; (b) the exposition of original texts
such as Stubbs Select Charters & medieval Latin chronicles, French &
German economists, Bluntschli, Voelkerrecht, the Madison Papers,
Elliotts Debates, Stat Laws, Records &c.

10. Sem. work consists of the individ. preparation & joint discussion
of original papers upon histor. & polit. subjects of the char. frequently
reported in the Univ. Circular. The best of these papers find their way
into the Univ. Studies or other special avenues for publica.

11. The natural outgrowth & highest requirement of the above system is a graduating thesis, wh must be a positive contribution to special
knowledge in the candidates chosen field.

The enviable reputation which Adams enjoyed increased
rapidly after 1884 because of his services in the organized
effort to gain recognition for the new profession of historical
scholars. In that year the American Historical Association
was founded and Adams became its secretary. As such he
more than anyone else arranged the programs of its annual
meetings, edited its publications, and generally directed its
affairs. Occupying this position he inevitably became one
of the leaders of the young and flourishing profession. By
the time of his resignation in 1900 from the strategic position
of secretary the new profession was firmly established. In
the intervening years the historical scholars of the new type
had been in great demand.

Adams was no exception and in the decade after 1883
received offer after offer. Among his papers is an envelope
on which Adams wrote "Chances in Other Colleges" and
underneath are listed twenty colleges and universities. The
correspondence included shows that in several cases only

tentative approaches were begun but in others persistent efforts were made to induce Adams to leave Baltimore. The offer which tempted Adams most was made in 1891, the same year he was promoted to a full professorship in the Johns Hopkins. It was to be professor of history in the new University of Chicago, head of that department and Dean of the Graduate School. Apparently the presidency of a state university did not tempt him, for he gave serious consideration to none of the several invitations extended to him.

These offers of administrative posts came to him because of his scholarly writing as well as because of his reputation as an organizer and promoter of research. The field in which he had worked chiefly in his first years at the Hopkins was American institutional history which meant the tracing of various local political institutions back to Germanic origins. It was evident that he had brought back to America more than a knowledge of German historical methods. Although these articles and monographs won applause both in America and Europe, at least from exponents of the Anglo-Saxon school of historical thought, they represented a brief phase in his career as a scholar. None was published after 1883. From then until his death most of his writings were on the subject of higher education in the United States. Some of them were on the new "scientific" methods in history or on the history of the study of history at this or that university. Others were devoted to the history of particular universities. This work brought him into close association with the United States Bureau of Education in Washington which published a number of his monographs. In 1887 he began to edit for the Bureau a series of "Contributions to American Educational History" and especially a series of histories of higher education in the various states. Many of the twenty-nine monographs of this character which were published before his death were written by graduates of his department. In all of his own writing in this field, even the most scholarly, a strong promotional spirit is clearly evident. Some of his briefer articles especially on university extension, a movement in which he became greatly interested, were frankly propagandist.[8] The most extended piece of historical writing Adams produced was in the same general field. This was his two volume *Life and Writings of Jared Sparks* (Boston, 1893) which he wrote at the request of the Sparks family.

It is a tribute to the scholarly ideals he instilled in his students that they never claimed, even in the memorial volume, that he was a great writer of scholarly history. He undoubtedly recognized his own limitations in that direction. Dr. Jameson, who was so closely associated with him, reported a conversation with Adams in which he said he had once planned to write a large history on the relations of church and state but realizing he could not also devote himself to his students chose the latter alternative. It was a wise decision. He had in rare proportions some of the qualities most desirable in a teacher. He always took a personal and generous interest in his students. A natural enthusiast himself, he imparted to them his enthusiasm for scholarly work. He seemed to have the faculty of bringing out the best that was in them. The finest scholars among his students—and no professor of history in the United States has yet had better—repeatedly testified to that effect.

---

[8] Anyone studying the history of university extension in the United States or of the Chautauqua movement can find helpful material in his letters.

The Idea of Scientific History in America

To THE STUDENT of American historiography there is no period comparable in interest to the last quarter of the nineteenth century and the early years of the twentieth. The achievements of the historians were remarkable. Moreover, two distinct forms of historical writing, the broad canvas and the miniature, flourished side by side. It was the golden age of the Titans who scaled the historical heaven by piling volume on volume. It was also the period during which the monograph, born of the new specialization, became the characteristic form of scholarly history. It was above all the period during which historical scholarship became a profession. At its beginning the writing and study of history in the United States had largely been the avocation of a few lawyers, clergy and business men. At its end there was a large and rapidly expanding group of university professors of history who had established a professional historical organization with a professional journal, and who showed commendable zeal in advancing the interests both of the profession and of scholarship. It was, moreover, a period of great interest because of the presence of certain ideas which either as an avowed philosophy or as unconscious prepossessions affected the history written.

Among these ideas was the belief generally shared by American scholars that history is a science. Such a conclusion was, of course, a natural one. Science had triumphed in the thought of the nineteenth century. To be "scientific" was the great desideratum. The very word was a fetish. So great was the prestige that the word "science" carried in academic circles that such monstrosities developed as "library science" and "domestic science." Even a new church based on ideas denying the validity of the fundamental principles upon which contemporary science rested took the name "Christian Science."

In conforming to the prevailing trend the historians paid high tribute to the dominance of the natural sciences by the way in which they identified their work with that which was acknowledged to be "pure science." Both because of its position in nineteenth-century thought and because of its obvious connection with mankind, biology was the science to which the historians most frequently turned. It furnished them with a terminology which they used again and again in their historical writing. In his famous essay on "The Significance of the Frontier in American History," which may well have been suggested by an application of Darwinism to history, Turner quickly stated his case in biological terms. "Behind institutions ... lie the vital forces which call these organs into life and shape them to meet changing conditions." The origins of American institutions, the "European germs," had been sufficiently emphasized and he proposed to show them adapting themselves to their new and constantly renewed environment, the American frontier.[1] Biology was associated

[1] Frederick Jackson Turner, "The Significance of the Frontier in American History," *Annual Report of the American Historical Association for 1893*, pp. 199, 201. Examples of biological terminology could be multiplied indefinitely, but one more coming from the professor under whom Turner studied must suffice. "This country will yet be viewed and reviewed as an

with history in another way. The new seminary method of training scholars, to which the scholarly renaissance was often attributed, was, according to a typical statement, "essentially the methods of biology applied to history."[2]

But history could claim kinship with other natural sciences too. Rhodes, in his address as president of the American Historical Association, said,"Even as the chemist and physicist, we talk of practice in the laboratory."[3] A professor of history made the point clearer. He hoped, he wrote, to establish "a sort of working historical laboratory for students, that shall correspond to chemical and physical laboratories, and where the process of learning shall be much the same,—not memorizing a text-book, but, so to speak, manipulating literary, political, and historical apparatus."[4] The same type of association but with still another natural science was noted by another scholar. "The Baltimore seminaries," he wrote, "are laboratories where books are treated like mineralogical specimens, passed about from hand to hand, examined, and tested."[5]

---

organism of historic growth, developing from minute germs, from the very protoplasm of state-life." Herbert B. Adams, "Cooperation in University Work," *Johns Hopkins University Studies in Historical and Political Science* (1883), I, 49.

[2] Francis N. Thorpe, "American History in Schools, Colleges and Universities," in H. B. Adams, *The Study of History in American Colleges and Universities,* p. 240. (U.S. Bureau of Education, Circular of Information No. 2, 1887.)

[3] James Ford Rhodes, "History," *Annual Report of the American Historical Association for 1899,* I, 48.

[4] The writer was Professor W. P. Atkinson of the Massachusetts Institute of Technology. W. Stull Holt, ed., *Historical Scholarship in the United States, 1876-1901; As Revealed in the Correspondence of Herbert B. Adams* (Baltimore, 1938), p. 63.

[5] *Ibid.,* p. 69 n. 1. The attention given by natural scientists to descriptions of their laboratory apparatus probably was responsible for the great emphasis Adams gave to the physical arrangement of the history seminar room. He had a diagram made, which he frequently published, showing the exact location of the seminar table, the various offices, the alcoves containing different periodicals and documents, etc. President Gilman evidently considered this important, for he asked Adams to send a copy of the diagram to Bishop Stubbs. *Ibid.*

It might reasonably be expected that the conception of history as a science would have been so fundamentally important to the historians that they would have discussed its every implication and have clarified its meaning. Such was not the case. The American historians displayed a curious reluctance to consider the question at all, as if they feared the effects of thought upon their resolution. Isolated references to history as one of the sciences or to their work as scientific can be found in abundance, but these give little or no inkling of what was meant. Occasionally an article was devoted directly to the subject. More frequently there would be some discussion of it by the scholar who happened to be president of the American Historical Association and who felt that in his presidential address some statement of historical faith was required. Yet even in these discussions it is often difficult to reconcile contradictory statements so as to ascertain what their authors conceived scientific history to be.

One thing is clear, however. All those who thought history was a science agreed in thinking that it had only recently become a science. There were two main schools of thought as to how history had become scientific. One attributed the transformation to the startling contemporary development of the natural sciences and especially of biology. "Those of us," wrote Henry Adams, "who read Buckle's first volume when it appeared in 1857, and almost immediately afterwards, in 1859, read the *Origin of Species* and felt the violent impulse which Darwin gave to the study of natural laws, never doubted that historians would follow until they had exhausted every possible hypothesis to create a science of history."[6] His brother, Charles Francis, also a historian in his own right, was still more certain that Darwin had already supplied the necessary theory. "On the first day of October, 1859," he

[6] Henry Adams, "The Tendency of History," *Annual Report of the American Historical Association for 1894*, pp. 17-18.

wrote, "the Mosaic cosmogony finally gave place to the Darwinian theory of evolution. Under the new dispensation, based not on chance or an assumed supernatural revelation, but on a patient study of biology, that record of mankind known as history, . . . has become a unified whole," and has ceased "to be a mere narrative, made up of disconnected episodes having little or no bearing on each other." Accordingly, 1859 was the date by which all historians must be tested. Gibbon, he continued, "was an orb of the first order; and it was his misfortune that he was born and wrote before Darwin gave to history unity and a scheme."[7]

The other and more numerous group ascribed the new dignity of history as a science not to any theory or discovery of natural scientists but to the ideal of complete objectivity which had been put within the scholar's reach by a recently perfected method. "It must be made clear," asserted Professor Emerton in an article explaining the new device, "that the claim of history to rank among sciences is founded in fact—the fact that it has a scientific method."[8] For this group the great figure was not the English scientist, Darwin, but the German historian, von Ranke. That is what Charles Kendall Adams meant when he said, "The modern scientific study of history everywhere has a tap-root running down into philology."[9] It was the philologists who had borrowed

[7] Charles Francis Adams, *The Sifted Grain and the Grain Sifters,* pp. 6, 31, 35, 36. Rhodes in 1899 had made the same point exactly; "History," pp. 48-49. See also, James Harvey Robinson, *The New History* (New York, 1913), pp. 43-44, 53. Much keener in analysis than anything written on this point by the Americans is the essay of the English historian, John B. Bury, "Darwinism and History," first published in 1909 and republished in *Selected Essays of J. B. Bury* (Cambridge, 1930), pp. 23-42.

[8] Ephraim Emerton, "The Historical Seminary in American Teaching," in G. Stanley Hall, *ed., Method of Teaching History* (Boston, 1883), p. 197.

[9] Charles Kendall Adams, "Recent Historical Work in the Colleges and Universities of Europe and America," *Annual Report of the American Historical Association for 1889,* p. 35. Yet in the introduction to his *Manual of Historical Literature* (New York, 1888), pp. 4-13, he seems to

the method from theological education, and it was as a member of philological seminaries that von Ranke became acquainted with its possibilities.[10] "The transformation of the *Seminarium* into a laboratory of science," an American scholar wrote, "was first accomplished more than fifty years ago by Germany's greatest historian, Leopold von Ranke." Through the influence of the students of "this father of historical science" the historical seminary was extended throughout Germany and the world.[11]

The science about whose origin there was this clash of opinion had different meanings for the American scholars of the period. From the vague allusions, the oblique comments, and the occasional clear statements, two distinct and contradictory conceptions of scientific history can be identified.

At one extreme was the belief that there were historical laws or generalizations which could be formulated. The essential characteristic of a science was the establishment of laws. Since human history lay entirely within a sphere in which the law of cause and effect has unrestricted dominion, and since it could therefore be reduced to general laws, it was a science. Such certainly was the view of George Bancroft when he told his young colleagues, "The movements of humanity are governed by law.... The character of science attaches to our pursuits."[12] On this point Bancroft, who had one of the simplest minds among the authors of

---

take the position that history not only isn't a science but cannot become one.

[10] Edward Gaylord Bourne, "Leopold von Ranke," *Annual Report of the American Historical Association for 1896*, I, 74 ff.

[11] Herbert B. Adams, "Methods of Historical Study," *Johns Hopkins University Studies in Historical and Political Science* (1884), II, 65.

[12] George Bancroft, "Self-Government," *Papers of the American Historical Association* (New York, 1888), II, 8. An obscure professor put the same conclusion in simpler language—"there is law in history; and history is a science," R. H. Dabney, "Is History a Science," *Papers of the American Historical Association* (New York, 1891), V, pt. 3, 86. On the other hand, the English-Canadian historian, Goldwin Smith, in his presidential

notable American histories, received the support of the historian who had the most complex and incisive mind in the group. Even before the last volumes of his famous history appeared, Henry Adams had become skeptical of the value of writing history as he and others were writing it. He foreshadowed his future activity and revealed his conception of scientific history by writing, "Should history ever become a true science, it must expect to establish its laws. . . ."[13] To formulate the laws of history was, he believed, the great challenge to the historians of the period. No better statement of this conception of scientific history and of its implications can be found than that in his address as President of the American Historical Association. "You may be sure," he wrote, "that four out of five serious students of history who are living today have, in the course of their work, felt that they stood on the brink of a great generalization that would reduce all history under a law as clear as the laws which govern the material world. . . . The law was certainly there, and as certainly was in places actually visible, to be touched and handled, as though it were a law of chemistry or physics. No teacher with a spark of imagination or with an idea of scientific method can have helped dreaming of the immortality that would be achieved by the man who should successfully apply Darwin's method to the facts of human history."[14]

At the other extreme from this meaning of scientific history,

address to the American Historical Association, denied that history was a science because free will and the part played by accidents precluded the possibility of law or of prediction. Goldwin Smith, "The Treatment of History," *American Historical Review* (April, 1905), X, 511-520.

[13] Henry Adams, *History of the United States* (New York, 1891), IX, 222.

[14] Henry Adams, "The Tendency of History," *Annual Report of the American Historical Association for 1894*, pp. 18-19. Some of those who talked in terms of historical laws were not clear on the question whether or not history was therefore a science. For example, Andrew D. White, the first president of the American Historical Association, referred to "the laws of general history" and cited a number of specific lessons or laws. Never-

which had obviously been suggested by the natural sciences, was the belief that scientific history consisted of a search for facts alone, with no laws or generalizations and with a renunciation of all philosophy. Thus, Rhodes, who once stressed the outstanding importance of Darwinian evolutionism for the historian, insisted later with equal finality that, since the object of the historian "is to tell a story and leave philosophy to others," his aim had been "to get rid so far as possible of all preconceived notions and theories."[15] Dunning stated the same idea in another way when he wrote, "The absorbing and relentless pursuit of the objective fact—of the thing that actually happened in exactly the form and manner of its happening, is . . . the typical function of the modern devotee of history."[16]

To be scientific was to be objective. To be objective was to study critically the genuine sources, and subsequently to describe impartially the facts of history with the same detached mind and in the same manner in which, it was believed, other scientists regarded natural phenomena. The facts, thus scientifically established without benefit of hypothesis or of generalization, would "speak for themselves." Interruptions by the historian were not regarded with favor. Henry C.

---

theless, he differentiated the study of history from the study of statistics by saying the latter was capable of "scientific proof" while the former was capable only of "moral proof." Andrew D. White, "On Studies in General History and the History of Civilization," *Papers of the American Historical Association* (New York, 1886), I, 7, 10, 13. James Schouler, on one occasion, wrote that "the stream of events," produced by the interaction of the human mind and its environment, "sweeps constantly onward, obedient to the law of moral gravity." Yet at another time he specifically condemned Buckle's attempt to reduce history to law and asserted, "There is no rigid scientific development to the human race." James Schouler, *History of the United States of America under the Constitution*, IV, 1. *Ibid.*, "Spirit of Research" in *Historical Briefs*, p. 24.

[15] M. A. De Wolfe Howe, *James Ford Rhodes; American Historian* (New York, 1929), pp. 149-150.

[16] William A. Dunning, "Truth in History," *American Historical Review* (January, 1914), XIX, 219.

Lea differed seriously with Lord Acton when the latter took the position that "the task of the historian is not simply to discover the truth and set it forth so that its lessons shall teach themselves."[17] Many obviously believed with Beveridge that "facts when justly arranged interpret themselves."[18] Yet even this interpretation was incidental, and the scientific historian need not concern himself with more than the establishment of the facts.

Before this conception of the science of history was accepted in America it had been widely disseminated in Europe. When his students applauded his historical proof that certain feudal institutions were Latin and not Germanic in origin, the French historian, Fustel de Coulanges, rebuked them, saying, "It is not I who speak, but history which speaks through me."[19] The Italian historian, Villari, expressed the theory in these words, "Let us assure our readers that we began and continued our work, throughout all our researches, and all our examinations of documents, without any preconceived ideas."[20] But it was the German, von Ranke, the acknowledged founder of this school of thought, who gave it its classical form, "Er [this work] will blos zeigen wie es eigentlich gewesen."[21]

[17] This was said in a review of Acton's, *A Lecture on the Study of History* published in the *American Historical Review* (April, 1896), I, 517. Note the apology in the following statement from the preface of a valuable historical work by an American scholar. "He [the author] has, therefore, except in a few instances where opinions were clearly warranted by the facts, confined himself to a simple statement of the truth and left the reader to form his own conclusions." James W. Garner, *Reconstruction in Mississippi* (New York, 1901), p. viii.

[18] Albert J. Beveridge, *Abraham Lincoln* (Boston, 1928), p. v.

[19] Quoted in Carl Becker, "Some Aspects of the Influence of Social Problems and Ideas upon the Study and Writing of History," *Publications of the American Sociological Society* (1913), VII, 94.

[20] Pasquale Villari, *The History of Girolamo Savonarola* (London, 1863), p. xxxiv.

[21] Leopold von Ranke, *Geschichten der romanischen und germanischen Völker von 1494 bis 1514,* p. vii.

It was to emulate von Ranke's scientific history that most of the Americans writing scholarly history after 1875 aspired. This was especially true of the group of professional historians who emerged during the period and quickly dominated the writing and study of history in the United States. Some of these attempted to bridge the gap between the two meanings of scientific history by suggesting that the objective facts when assembled might, in speaking for themselves, enunciate a law. Professor Hart, revealing what must have been a widespread misconception of the methods employed by scholars in the natural sciences, explained how scientific historians concerned only with objective facts might at the same time establish historical laws. "For such a process," he wrote, "we have the fortunate analogy of the physical sciences: did not Darwin spend twenty years in accumulating data, and in selecting typical phenomena, before he so much as ventured a generalization? . . . In history, too, scattered and apparently unrelated data fall together in harmonious wholes; the mind is led to the discovery of laws; and the explorer into scientific truth is at last able to formulate some of those unsuspected generalizations which explain the whole framework of the universe."[22]

In spite of this and similar attempts to be in both camps there can be no doubt that the proponents of such views adhered to the "objective-facts" theory of scientific history, even though they considered their allegiance temporary. This was made clear by another American historian. No better statement of the faith dominating two generations of American scholars can be found than the following passage from the presidential address of George Burton Adams:

At the very beginning of all conquest of the unknown lies the fact, established and classified to the fullest extent possible at the moment.

[22] A. B. Hart, "Imagination in History," *American Historical Review* (January, 1910), XV, 232-233.

To lay such foundations, to furnish such materials for later builders, may be a modest ambition, but it is my firm belief that in our field of history, for a long time to come, the man who devotes himself to such labors, who is content with this preliminary work, will make a more useful and a more permanent contribution to the final science, or philosophy of history, than will he who yields to the allurements of speculation and endeavors to discover in the present stage of our knowledge the forces that control society, or to formulate the laws of their action. None of the new battle cries should sound for us above the call of our first leader, proclaiming the chief duty of the historian to establish *wie es eigentlich gewesen. . . .* The field of the historian is, and must long remain, the discovery and recording of what actually happened.[23]

There is much evidence to show that Professor Adams was speaking for a majority of his American colleagues. In the first place, their education had been based on this assumption of the nature of scholarly history. Most of them had been trained in the seminars which had spread rapidly throughout the country and which diffused, in fact although not of necessity, von Ranke's conception of history along with his method. Secondly, there are the specific statements of these views which were sometimes made, usually with the emphasis on the discovery of "the facts" as the sole end of the historian's work, but on occasion with a frank denial of the presence of any theory or philosophy of history. Generally, however, the Americans said nothing on the subject. The paucity of discussion suggests either that they considered the matter obvious or, what is more likely, they were unaware of the assumptions and concepts which in fact formed the theory of historiography they employed. Yet if they did not write on this subject they did write history, and their books offer the best evidence of their theory. No one can analyze

[23] George Burton Adams, "History and the Philosophy of History," *American Historical Review* (January, 1909), XIV, 236.

much of the scholarly history written, especially the monographs of the professionals, without appreciating the extent
to which they were dominated by von Ranke's ideal.

The full effects of the two conceptions of scientific history
on the history written in the United States have never been
thoroughly described, nor will an attempt be made to do
so here. But several important conclusions are clear. The
law-in-history school of thought has proven barren. The
unrelenting search for "a great generalization that would
reduce all history under a law," which Henry Adams con-
fidently predicted fifty years ago, has, in fact, never material-
ized. The occasions when a student of history in America
has seriously occupied himself with an attempt to formulate
a historical law have been rare indeed, and the fruits of
these attempts have neither interested nor satisfied the other
historians.[24] Similar failure attended the few efforts to write
history in terms of law.[25] Generalizations regarding the historical process were, of course, inevitably employed in all
the history written, but they were either employed uncon-
sciously or were regarded as so obvious as to need no critical
examination. The instances in which a generalization has
been deliberately adopted with a warning to the reader that
it will determine the selection and organization of the facts
can literally be counted on the fingers of one hand. The
consequences of the other school of scientific history have
been tremendous. Most of the scholarly history written in
the United States from 1875 to the present has been conceived
in terms of objective facts. The value put on the facts as

[24] The most systematic and sophisticated effort was, of course, that of
Henry Adams himself. The tentative and unsatisfactory nature of the con-
clusions of a scholar more typical of the historians, who untypically had
the temerity to grapple with the problem, can be seen in Edward P.
Cheyney, "Law in History," *American Historical Review* (January, 1924),
XXIX, 231-248.

[25] Perhaps the best examples would be the historical writings of John
W. Draper and of Brooks Adams.

an end in themselves; the emphasis given to the establishment of facts; the fear of making any statements without a supporting document; the belief, sometimes avowed, that complete objectivity could be attained merely by honest effort; the denial of any philosophy and theory of history in the prepossession that historians should, or could, be without prepossessions—all testify to the same conclusion.

This conception of scientific history, which dominated scholars both in Europe and in America, was certain to share the common fate of all ideas. Critical attacks challenged its validity. With poetic justice, they apparently started and certainly have received their fullest development in von Ranke's own country. From Germany they spread to America. After the turn of the century a number of American scholars began to undermine the prevailing theory.[26] The form the attack took was to point out that the prevailing theory was a theory and to make explicit the assumptions implicit in it. It was not until 1935, however, that an American, frankly summarizing the work accumulated by German scholarship, stated fully the elements and assumptions of the faith in objective scientific history.[27] The first is that the facts

[26] Among the noteworthy examples are: Fred Morrow Fling, "Historical Synthesis," *American Historical Review* (October, 1903), IX, 1-22; the writings of Frederick J. Teggart, especially "The Circumstance or the Substance of History," *American Historical Review* (July, 1910), XV, 709-719, and *Prolegomena to History* (Berkeley, 1916); James Harvey Robinson, *The New History* (New York, 1913); the more incisive and provocative work of Carl Becker, especially, in addition to the article already cited, "Everyman His Own Historian," *American Historical Review* (January, 1932), XXXVII, 221-236; and Charles A. Beard, "Written History as an Act of Faith," *American Historical Review* (January, 1934), 219-229; *Discussion of Human Affairs* (New York, 1936); Charles A. Beard and Alfred Vagts, "Currents in Historiography," *American Historical Review* (April, 1937), XLII, 460-483. A counter-attack on what he calls historical relativism can be found in Maurice Mandelbaum, *The Problem of Historical Knowledge* (New York, 1938).

[27] Charles A. Beard, "That Noble Dream," *American Historical Review* (October, 1935), XLI, 74-87.

of history have existed as an object or series of objects outside
the mind of the historian. The second is that the historian can
know this object or series of objects and can describe it as it
objectively existed. This involves the question of documentation, the only way in which a historian can observe the facts.
But documentation can only cover a small fraction of the
events of history. This also requires the historian to divest
himself of all philosophical, religious, political, economic,
social, sex, moral and aesthetic interests so that he can view
the facts with strict impartiality. It also presupposes that the
facts can be grasped by a purely rational or intellectual process. A final major assumption is that the facts of history
have some structural organization through inner, perhaps
causal, relations which any impartial historian can ascertain
and on which all must agree.

The challenging of these assumptions has raised the most
crucial problem confronting contemporary historiography in
all its branches. If the challenge is not successfully met, the
period of "scientific history" in America will be definitely
ended. The challenge itself, however, is, in the main, the
application to the business of the historiographer of preconceptions which are primarily philosophical and psychological
in their content and origins, and about which no generally
accepted verdict can as yet be said to have been rendered.
Nevertheless, whatever the outcome, the previously current
conceptions of "scientific history" must be modified and, as
the historians are compelled to consider the nature of the
foundations on which their historical constructions rest, a
more sophisticated scholarship must inevitably result.

Historical Scholarship in the Twentieth Century

HISTORICAL SCHOLARSHIP, like other branches of thought and human activity, is inevitably integrated with the society of which it is a part. There may occasionally be an individual scholar significantly out of touch with the time and place in which he is working. Thus Richard Hildreth departed so far from many of the prevailing assumptions of the middle of the nineteenth century that his major historical work received little attention, although forty years later, in the 1880's and 1890's and in a more favorable climate of opinion it was generally regarded as the outstanding example of historical scholarship by an American. Such exceptions do not invalidate the generalization that there is always a close connection between the historical scholarship of any period and the fundamental prepossessions and characteristics of the society in which the scholars are living.

This nexus is economic as well as ideological. Scholarly activity, if not a luxury, depends nevertheless upon the support which its nourishing society can or will give it. Consequently perhaps the first fact to record in a consideration of historical scholarship in the first half of the twentieth century is that the United States during those fifty years has gone through an amazing economic development and has amassed wealth unequalled by any other people during the same or any other period. The statistics showing the increase in the annual production of iron and steel, of coal, of wheat, and of manufactured goods reveal a process that literally staggers the imagination. Yet large as they are, they are surpassed by the rate of increase in the number of students attending colleges and universities. In 1900 these numbered 238,000, or approximately the ratio of one student to 323 persons in the total population. By 1950 the number of students had reached 2,500,000, and the ratio of students to total population was one to 60. Whatever may be thought of this increase in the percentage of students seeking training beyond the level of secondary education, it is a product of the increasing complexity of a civilization in which the specialist is of prime importance, of the vast increase in national wealth, and of the ideal that education to the limit of his capacities is the right of every citizen and that the diffusion of appropriate training is basic to the welfare of the nation.

Naturally scholarship in all fields has been affected by this development. Whether or not historical scholarship received a fair portion of the national investment in post-high school education or even relatively as large a share as in earlier and poorer days, there can be no doubt of the vast increase in the support given. To appreciate the truth of this, one has only to compare the library resources available in 1900 with those of 1950, when there are three or four dozen libraries larger and better in quality than the best of 1900. The Harvard University library, which had just under 600,000 volumes in 1900, had expanded to over 5,000,000 by the middle of the century. Others grew at comparable rates. More significant than mere growth in size was the increasing emphasis given to university libraries as centers for research and the appearance of distinctively research libraries. While the gradual and unheralded increase of materials for research in nearly every university library had more effect on scholarship, the establishment of special research libraries dramatized the process. Among the latter the Hoover Library on War, Revolution, and Peace at Stanford University, the William L. Clements Library of American History at the University of Michigan, and the Henry E. Huntington Library at San Marino, California, deservedly received much publicity.

Perhaps the best illustration of the way in which private philanthropy and government combined to facilitate historical scholarship was the project for the reproduction of materials in foreign archives relating to American history. In 1927 Mr. John D. Rockefeller, Jr., gave half a million dollars to the Library of Congress for such a purpose. After that sum was exhausted the Library of Congress from another philanthropic fund and from moneys appropriated to it by Congress continued the project so that by 1940 there were in the Library some three million pages of manuscript documents in the shape of photostats and especially of microfilms. Thus for many subjects the scholar in the middle of the twentieth century does not have to rely on handwritten transcripts or notes nor does he have to travel from archive to archive in foreign countries, as did the scholars of the nineteenth century. In spite of these great advantages very little of this vast deposit of scholarly ore has as yet been refined into historical works.

Other benefits to historical scholarship resulting from the increased wealth in America have come from private philanthropy which that wealth made possible. These are the grants-in-aid, the fellowships, and the various subsidies which are now available and which were almost nonexistent in 1900.

Literally dozens of fellowships have been endowed in the leading graduate schools of the country to encourage scholarly work and there are, of course, the larger and better known grants made by the Social Science Research Council, the American Council of Learned Societies, the Guggenheim Foundation, and many others.

But the best index of the relation between the economic development of America and historical scholarship can be found in the number of professors of history who are fed, clothed, and sheltered, not of course in the style which they would prefer or which they perhaps deserve, but at least on a scale which permits them to engage in scholarly work. Not all members of the guild have been or are scholars, yet historical scholarship throughout the first half of the twentieth century has been in the custody of this professional group. On a very few occasions the field has been successfully invaded by nonprofessionals like Senator Beveridge or the early James Truslow Adams, both of them men whose scholarly abilities have been readily acclaimed by the profession. Instances of this kind have, however, been rare. Consequently, any account of historical scholarship in America from 1900 to 1950 must be focused on the professional group upon whose ideas, vision, standards, and methods the fate of that body of knowledge depended.

In the transit of a science or an art from one civilization to another a number of stages have been distinguished. In the first the sole practitioners of the art or science in the country are aliens. During the second stage there are native practitioners who have been educated abroad. The third stage is reached when natives are educated in the field of knowledge at home in schools whose faculties are composed of aliens or natives who have been trained abroad. In the last stage marking the final transition of the art or science to the new country natives are taught by natives who have been educated at home. Perhaps a further development can be noted if the new country surpasses the old and persons from the old center of civilization must seek training and knowledge in the new country.

By 1900 the profession of historical scholarship was in the third stage of its transit from western Europe. Forty years earlier there had been no such profession and the few historians in the country were lawyers or clergy or gentlemen with leisure to devote to their avocation of studying and writing history. Twenty years earlier the new profession emerged in the persons of eleven professors of history. Between 1880 and 1900 the profession became firmly established. There were at the beginning of the new century something over one hundred professors of history and more significantly there were a number of graduate schools for the training of new recruits. The instructors in these schools were native Americans many or most of whom had studied in Europe. They and their students, for obvious and professional reasons, had in 1884 created a national organization, the American Historical Association, and in 1895 they launched the professional journal, *The American Historical Review*.[1]

The new profession could not have been established at a more favorable time nor in a more favorable society. The phenomenal increase in the number of students from 1900 to 1950 necessitated a corresponding expansion of faculty to instruct them. At present there are approximately 7,500 professional historians, the vast majority of whom are teachers of history rather than scholars who also contribute to knowledge by writing history. The professional training of such numbers has been possible only because a considerable number of

[1] H. Hale Bellot, "Some Aspects of the Recent History of American Historiography," *Transactions of the Royal Historical Society,* Fourth Series, XXVIII (1946), 120-148. W. Stull Holt (ed.), *Historical Scholarship in the United States, 1876-1901: As Revealed in the Correspondence of Herbert B. Adams* (Baltimore, Md.: The Johns Hopkins Press, 1938).

American colleges became universities where graduate work was offered and where scholarly attainments, especially in research, were the criteria for appointments and promotions. Rightly or wrongly the same training and the same standards of appointment have been employed for college teachers. Throughout the period various people have argued that the preparation for the Ph.D. degree, by requiring so much concentration of research from men who are unlikely to engage in research after leaving graduate school, has prevented the students from getting the broad scholarly knowledge essential for good college teachers. In spite of repeated protests of this nature the program of graduate training in history has retained the emphasis on research. In fact there is probably greater weight attached to research now than there was fifty years ago. At least the prevailing standards for doctoral dissertations have come to demand a much more extensive piece of research than would formerly have been accepted. There is truth in the gibe that the graduate students write books while the professors write articles. Whatever the merits of the arguments about the program for the Ph.D. degree, it is clear that long before the middle of the century Americans wishing to enter the profession of historical scholarship could receive, and regularly did receive, the necessary training in American graduate schools staffed by Americans who had themselves been educated in America. The science of history, to give it the name most used in the early years of the twentieth century, had been successfully transplanted from its European source. There is, however, little evidence that the stage has been reached where Europeans feel compelled to come to America because they recognize a superior or richer standard of historical scholarship, except, of course, in the specially favored field of the history of the United States.

If the new professional group in America has flourished and prospered since 1900, what can be said of historical scholarship whose fate was in the hands of the group? Certain results are obvious. There has been great activity, specialization, elaborate organization, a much higher level of technical scholarly standards, a few distinctive schools of interpretation, and a growing interest in basic conceptions.

Members of a professional group, in America at least, seem to feel a need for many organizations. The historians were no exception to this rule. Their rapid expansion in numbers, the tendency to narrow specialization as more thorough research has led to fragmentation of even such a subject as history, and other obvious professional considerations have led to the creation of a multiplicity of organizations. In nearly every instance one principal objective, certainly one consequence of the organization, has been the publication of a scholarly journal. The American Council of Learned Societies, itself an illustration of one type of scholarly organization, has published at five-year intervals *A List of American Learned Journals Devoted to Humanistic and Social Studies.* In that of 1945, there are listed 86 journals under History, all except a handful started in the twentieth century. In addition to these there are many others under other categories which are essentially historical in character, like the *Journal of the History of Ideas* under Philosophy or the *Journal of Economic History* under Economics, to mention only two. The titles of these journals, each of which has a separate scholarly organization sponsoring it, illustrate the wide range of subjects in which American scholars have specialized. The following is a random selection: *Journal of Modern History, Byzantion* (The Byzantine Institute), *Speculum* (The Mediaeval Academy), *Agricultural History, The Hispanic American Historical Review, Isis* (History of Science Society), *Journal of Negro History, Journal of Southern History, Church History, Catholic Historical Review, Military Affairs, Bulletin of the Business Historical Society,* and the *Mississippi Valley Historical Review.*

In nearly every one of the American States there is a historical society which publishes a journal. The members of these societies are predominantly not professional scholars but in the vast majority of cases the journals are now edited by local representatives of the professional group and the articles published are written by professionals. The amateur local historian so typical of the nineteenth century is conspicuously absent and the scholarly value of the history published is as conspicuously increased.

Although there are many important ways in which this intensive organization of scholarly work has contributed to historical scholarship by preventing wasted effort, by raising standards, by facilitating research, and by making possible such a notable achievement as the *Dictionary of American Biography,* it must nevertheless be emphasized that great history cannot be organized into being. There are also some positive disadvantages which have been realized from the process. Some men of genuine talent have been lured into devoting their lives to organizing scholarship rather than to using it creatively. By common consent J. Franklin Jameson was among the most distinguished of American historical scholars in the first half of the twentieth century. Many would say that no American surpassed him in breadth of learning, or in scholarly wisdom. The few small pieces of historical work of his own which he published indicate what might have been had he not dedicated his abilities of a high order to organizing scholarship, to editing journals for the work of lesser minds, to publishing documents, to preparing and administering the preparation of bibliographies and other aids to scholarship.[2]

When he denied himself the real work of the historian, Jameson was acting on the theory generally accepted by the

[2] A memoir describing his life and achievements was published in the journal he edited for so many years. "John Franklin Jameson," *American Historical Review,* XLIII (January, 1938), 243-252.

profession in the early years of the century, if not later, that the great task confronting historical scholars was to assemble as many firmly established facts as possible, leaving their use to the scholars of the future. Many seemed to think that when a sufficiently large pile of bricks should be gathered they would arrange themselves into a beautiful and useful building. Others appreciated the fact that an architect would be necessary but with too much modesty expected that the scholar of the future would be able to do what they considered beyond their capacity and dared not attempt. Fortunately for their peace of mind it did not occur to them that the future builder might use some other material than the bricks they were piling, might ask completely different questions of the past and therefore need different facts. Meanwhile prestige and scholarly reputation were to be won, since the editing of documents and similar brick piling activities conformed to the prevailing canons of the profession.

The specialization born of the more intensive standards of scholarship and so closely related to the elaborate organization of scholarship brought significant changes in the form of the history written. Prior to the twentieth century the dominant type of the best histories was the extensive treatment by one author of a large subject in many volumes. Several of these painters on huge canvases overlapped the twentieth century. A few of them whose volumes were all published after 1900 do not present real exceptions to this statement. Thus Channing had begun his huge work before the turn of the century, and it is perhaps not grossly unfair to E. Raymond Turner to suggest that his volumes on the Cabinet Council and the Privy Council, like Osgood's on the American Colonies, approximated collections of data rather than histories. The outstanding example of multivolumed scholarly history conceived and executed in the twentieth century is the work of Lawrence Gipson which has now reached the seventh of the

contemplated twelve volumes. Other exceptions are the extended work of Louis Gottschalk on Lafayette of which four
volumes have so far appeared and the seven volumes of Douglas Freeman on Lee and his lieutenants.

These instances constitute rare exceptions and no observers
would deny that in the twentieth century, and under the mo-
nopoly of historical scholarship by the professionals, the characteristic form of historical writing has been the monograph.
The reasons for the dominance of the monograph are obvious,
as are its chief benefits. Yet if much was gained in terms of
thorough research and of intensive and critical use of materials, much also may have been lost. Too many monographs
have revealed superior scholarly abilities being wasted on
inferior and insignificant subjects. One wonders even in the
case of the most valuable monographic work if a still greater
contribution could not have been made through the extensive
form. For example consider the cases of Carl Becker and
Henry Adams. Their talents were similar and preëminent.
Becker was certainly the equal of Adams in his mastery of
scholarly techniques; he had a comparable, incisive mind; he,
too, probed deeply into human action while viewing events
with philosophical calm, and his literary power equaled as
well as resembled that of Adams. It is probably correct to say
that Becker's miniatures, brilliant as they are, will not have the
lasting qualities of the large canvas of Henry Adams nor have
they made as significant a contribution to historical scholarship in America.

One result of the adoption of the monograph as the vehicle
for scholarly work has been the development of coöperative
histories. Events and human activities stubbornly refuse to
atomize themselves into small units of monographic size. And
human minds, including those of the scholars themselves,
refuse to be satisfied with fragments, wanting larger syntheses
than can be included in a monograph or the complete story of

a theme too large to be circumscribed by a monograph. The solution which became a characteristic feature in American, as well as European, scholarship has been a coöperative work. Sometimes the coöperation takes the form of a series of volumes, each a monograph by a specialist in the particular subject or period. Unity and coherence in the entire work depend on the editor or editors who plan the project and are responsible for whatever integration is possible. The success, both scholarly and commercially, of the 26-volume *American Nation Series* of 1904-1907 encouraged other attempts. The most notable have been the Yale *Chronicles of America* (50 volumes), *The History of American Life* (13 volumes), *The Rise of Modern Europe* (20 volumes in progress), *A History of the South* (10 volumes in progress), *The Economic History of the United States* (9 volumes in progress). Since ventures of this size are expensive, they have usually been devoted to the history of the United States, as that is the field of history most likely to be bought by the American public. Sometimes the coöperative work results from the combination of separate articles by different authors in the various volumes. Such for example is Tenney Frank's *Economic Survey of the Roman Empire*, the five volumes of which contain sections written by various American and European scholars. Such also is the ten-volume work, *The American Secretaries of State and Their Diplomacy*, edited by S. F. Bemis and written by thirty-nine American scholars.

These attempts to supply histories on large themes while retaining the advantages of the monographs by specialists have not been attended by notable success. The standards of intensive research have usually been preserved in the separate parts of volumes, but the total picture has lacked unity, coherence, and proportion. Apparently in historical work the best results can be obtained only when one mind studies all the data and erects the entire structure. Perhaps this is saying that the writing of history is in some respects a work of art and like a symphony must be the creation of one man. Certainly the history of historical writing both in Europe and America shows no coöperative work equal to the achievements of individuals. The separate monographs may each be a scholarly jewel but when they are put together the resulting mosaic is a disappointing or drab affair.

The monographs of the new professional scholars in America were by specialists and for specialists. Scholarly history in the twentieth century was not read by the public to the same extent as the scholarly history of earlier periods. This fact did not disturb the scholars in the early years of the century. Indeed they saw in it cause for satisfaction. In their desire to be scientific and in their aversion to predecessors whom they scornfully labeled "literary historians" they deliberately shunned a felicitous literary style which might encourage reading by the public. The cold and unadorned style of a laboratory report fitted more closely their theory of history as a science. A case has been noted in which a scholar stated, by implication at least, that the historical work he was considering might be esteemed as good (that is, scientific) history if only it had been badly written.[3] Naturally the public, not being under professional compulsion to read the monographs or journals, did not do so.

One fact must be recorded to the credit of the historical scholars. They have at no time created and used a specialized

[3] The comment is that of John Spencer Bassett on Francis Parkman in *The Middle Group of American Historians* (New York: Macmillan, 1917), p. ix. Bassett wrote: "While he [Parkman] wrote with that full appreciation of style which was characteristic of Bancroft and the literary historians, his industry, his research among documents, and especially his detachment seem to place him among the men of to-day." Carl Becker in a delightful and penetrating essay, "Labelling the Historians," quoted this sentence and observed "If Parkman had only written badly, no one could question his scientific standing." *Everyman His Own Historian* (New York: F. S. Crofts and Co., 1935), p. 135.

or technical terminology. In thus refusing to follow the example of scholars in most branches of knowledge, including economics, sociology, psychology, philosophy, and education, to mention only a few, the historians denied themselves some advantages. The general public, as well as colleagues in the academic world, could not be impressed by an awesome vocabulary, incomprehensible to all save the initiated. More importantly, the historians lacking specially designed words have employed those commonly used and hence often loosely used. Words like "cause" or "fact" have, in fact, caused a lot of trouble. Offsetting these disadvantages is the one great gain. If the historians have anything of moment to say and if they can say it with even a modicum of literary art, the public will be able to understand it. Admittedly, the scholars in history at the beginning of the century were not taking advantage of this opportunity and were out of touch with the reading public.

Gradually during the twentieth century the profession became dissatisfied with this situation, against which there had always been a few protestants. The cause of the change in attitude was neither a desire for royalties, nor pressure from commercial publishers, since the latter willingly left the publication of historical monographs to the rapidly expanding university presses. To some extent the scholars began to take less seriously the theory of history as science, a theory which tended to make history dull. Greater weight can be assigned to World War I, which stimulated nationalism and which confronted members of the historical profession, some through direct personal experience, with the problem of making historical knowledge more directly useful to the American people. One conclusion quickly reached was that scholarly knowledge had been kept too largely within the small circle of scholars. The obvious remedy was to write scholarly history in a way that the public would read. An effort to do precisely that resulted in the Yale *Chronicles* series which appeared immediately after World War I. In these small volumes, footnotes and all the apparatus of scholarship disappeared, and deliberate efforts were made to present sound scholarly knowledge in an attractive literary style. In the second quarter of the century the new attitude won general acceptance, and more and more of the monographic work came to be written if not with literary art at least with greater effectiveness than formerly.

When throughout the period people lamented the gulf between scholarly knowledge and the public, one important consideration regularly escaped attention. If the general public refused to buy the scholarly history being written, a special and growing public was brought into contact with historical scholarship by a different path. These were the men and women who went to colleges and universities where most of them were likely to attend a course in history. The college population increased so rapidly that before 1950 statistics showed that about 30 per cent of the graduates from high school continued their education in an institution of higher learning. What proportion of them actually took any courses in history cannot be stated with any exactness but it must have been large enough to include a significant section of the total population. Thus through spoken history in lectures and through directed reading many more of the population probably had some contact with historical scholarship than several generations earlier when people bought scholarly histories because they were enjoyable.

The writing of textbooks loomed large among the activities of the professional scholars. In no other country could so many and such good textbooks be found, probably because in no other country were there such numbers of university students to buy them. The rewards for the author of a successful book have been large both in money and in prestige. It is an unflattering comment on the scholarly standards of the profession that the writing of textbooks should bring prestige since they so seldom contain either new knowledge or original interpretations. Yet such is the case, and more than one distinguished reputation as a scholar has been based primarily on a widely used textbook. In some cases—Channing's was one —a textbook has provided the author with funds necessary for original investigation and genuine contributions. It can mean freedom from servitude in summer schools, thus enabling the author to escape that menace to productive scholarship. More often the textbook itself acts as one of the gravest dangers to historical scholarship. Every large publishing house wishes to have a textbook for every course in history given in several institutions. To increase sales a new edition or an entirely different book is brought out every few years. Consequently temptation has been constantly placed before the more promising members of the profession and they have succumbed with little resistance. Far too much of the time and energy of the profession in the twentieth century has been diverted to a needless multiplication of textbooks, leaving not enough for the production of scholarly work of the type which the future will not willingly let die.[4]

II

Professional scholars, like all historians of all times and places, subscribe to some theory or make some assumptions, avowed or unavowed, of the nature and limits of historiography. These ideas will inevitably determine the character of the history written. Although the American scholars of the nineteenth century and of the early years of the twentieth displayed a curious reluctance to consider what they were doing

[4] Next to nothing has been written on the history of the writing of textbooks. Almost the only valuable account, although restricted to one important example, can be found in Eric F. Goldman, *John Bach McMaster* (Philadelphia: University of Pennsylvania Press, 1943).

or what were their philosophical preconceptions, they undoubtedly subscribed to the belief that history is a science. Such a conclusion was a natural one. Science had triumphed in the thought of the nineteenth century. To be "scientific" was the great desideratum. The very word was a fetish. So great was the prestige that the word "science" carried in the academic world that such verbal monstrosities appeared as "library science" and "domestic science." Even a new church based on ideas denying the validity of the fundamental principles upon which contemporary science rested took the name "Christian Science."

Under these circumstances it was not extraordinary that the emerging vigorous professional historical group should think of themselves as scientists and their subject of study as science. The science of history meant to a small minority the establishment of laws or generalizations. This conception of historical science proved to be barren, for little or no history was written under the influence of this conception. To the vast majority of American scholars scientific history meant the search for objective facts alone, with no laws or generalizations and with a renunciation of all philosophy. To be scientific was to be objective. To be objective was to study critically the sources and to ascertain impartially the facts of history, as they actually happened ("wie es eigentlich gewesen"). This was to be done with the same detached mind and in the same manner in which, it was believed, natural scientists observed their phenomena. The objective facts, thus established by a completely neutral historian-scientist without benefit of generalization or any preconceptions, would speak for themselves. Nearly all of the scholarly history written in the United States in the late nineteenth and in the first half of the twentieth century was written under the influence of this basic conception. The high value put on facts as an end in themselves; the emphasis given to the establishment of facts; the fear of venturing any statement without a supporting document; the belief, occasionally avowed, that complete objectivity could be attained merely by honest effort; the denial of any philosophy or theory of history in the assumption that historians should, or could, be without prepossessions; and the very literary style of their writing all testify to the vast influence of the "objective facts" theory of scientific history.[5]

Not long after the turn of the century critics challenged the validity of this school of thought. With poetic justice the challenges received their fullest development in Germany, from where the conception of history as science had spread throughout western civilization, although non-Germanic thinkers, like Croce, also led in the attack. Traditionally, Americans have manifested little interest in the fundamental propositions on which their field of knowledge rested and at first only a few rare scholars even knew that the prevailing historical faith was under scrutiny. But by the fourth decade of the century the writings of Carl Becker and Charles A. Beard raised the issue before the profession and a heated controversy developed.

The critics insisted that the prevailing theory of objective scientific history was a theory and insisted on making explicit the assumptions implicit in it. The first assumption, they pointed out, is that the facts of history have existed as an object or series of objects outside the mind of the historian. The second is that the historian can know this object or series and can describe it as it objectively existed. This involves the question of documentation, the only way in which the historian can observe the facts. Yet documentation can only cover a

---

[5] Some of these points are elaborated in W. Stull Holt, "The Idea of Scientific History in America," *Journal of the History of Ideas,* I (June, 1940), 352-362; reprinted in this volume. An excellent, if somewhat illogically arranged, bibliography of the literature bearing on this and several subsequent paragraphs is in *Theory and Practice in Historical Study: A Report of the Committee on Historiography,* Social Science Research Council Bulletin 54 (1946).

small fraction of the events of history. This also requires the historian to divest himself of all philosophical, religious, political, economic, sexual, moral, and aesthetic interests so that he can view the facts with strict impartiality. It also presupposes that the facts can be grasped by a purely rational process. The final assumption is that the facts of history have some structural organization through inner or causal relations which any impartial historian can ascertain and on which all must agree.[6]

With remarkable ease and speed the old historical faith to which American historians had adhered for so long was abandoned. Undoubtedly the intellectual climate of opinion was hostile to absolutes in all fields of thought. Perhaps the same attitude which resulted in relativity in the physical sciences accounted for the new conception of history. Certainly the label used supports that conclusion, for the new historical faith is called historical relativism. How widely it has been accepted cannot as yet be stated, but it seems to have gained many converts. A Committee on Historiography, composed of eight scholars widely and favorably known in the profession, submitted a report in 1946 in which relativism was embraced.[7] It is too soon to discern the consequences of the new ideas concerning the nature of the foundations on which historical writing and scholarship rest. That they will be far reaching and fundamental must be expected.

Some other assumptions which affect historical scholarship have also been subjected to analysis especially during the latter part of the half century. One of these is the idea of progress

[6] Charles A. Beard, "That Noble Dream," *American Historical Review*, XLI (October, 1935), 74-87.

[7] The title of the report is given in note 5 above. The philosophy of history accepted by the Committee can be found in the Propositions presented as those on which the branch of knowledge known as history rests. See also, Charles W. Cole, "The Relativity of History," *Political Science Quarterly*, XLVIII (June, 1933), 161-171.

which influenced powerfully the thinking of nearly all Americans, including those who wrote history, down to or past World War I. The characteristic optimism resulting from the rapid growth of the country and from the prosperity of its people combined with the interpretation put upon the science of the nineteenth century to persuade Americans that the concept of progress was valid.[8] Either the devastating impact of World War I or currents of thought from abroad, reaching historical scholarship directly by such works as Spengler's *Decline of the West*, profoundly altered this article of faith. When one writes of particular people at a particular time and place, as historians must, and when monographic treatment further limits the range of thought, demonstrations of progress are not likely to emerge. Yet professions of belief in progress can readily be found in the works of nineteenth-century scholars, sometimes scattered profusely in the narrative as in the histories of George Bancroft and John Fiske, more often stated in a preface. Thus Edward Channing in the Preface to the first volume of his great work published in 1905 avowed his belief in history as "the story of living forces, always struggling onward and upward toward that which is better and higher in human conception." As the twentieth century advanced, belief in progress became increasingly difficult to maintain and increasingly rare in historical writing. In fact, much more typical were the sentences with which a young scholar, Robert R. Palmer, concluded his *A History of the Modern World*, published in 1950. In them he somewhat grimly clings to the hope that if our civilization fails in the current cataclysm another would rise in its place.

Among other basic ideas circumscribing historical scholarship have been nationalism, liberalism, pragmatism, democ-

---

[8] Some of the reasons for the widespread American belief in progress are discussed in the Introduction by Charles A. Beard to the American edition of J. B. Bury, *The Idea of Progress* (New York: Macmillan, 1932).

racy, capitalism, and the belief that man is primarily a rational being. Nearly all have been challenged and subjected to critical analysis rather than being taken for granted as formerly. The tremendous significance of nationalism in the modern world came to be appreciated after World War I and with greater understanding more and more history was written in those terms. Even in writing the history of their own nation American scholars have displayed a sophistication in marked contrast with the uncritical naïveté with which earlier generations had used what is now called "the Anglo-Saxon legend."

Less scholarly analysis has been given to liberalism and democracy in spite of the challenges from totalitarian ideas in the second quarter of the century. The influence of these concepts on historical scholarship has been vast. The most conservative of American historians could not escape from the liberal, democratic tradition of which they were a part. The result was that the worth and liberty of the individual person and of democracy as the proper way of organizing society was accepted as axiomatic. The same forces and ideas which produced the Progressive movement with its belief that the cure for the weaknesses of democracy is more democracy gave a Progressive coloring to the histories written in America. This climate of opinion has lasted longer in scholarly circles than in the political sphere.

Everyone who writes or studies history must confront the problem of human behavior and must accordingly hold, either avowedly or unavowedly, basic conceptions regarding psychology. In 1900 there can be little doubt that the historians in America shared the prevailing view that man was essentially a rational being. Some psychologists, notably Freud, had already begun to stress the role of the unconscious and the irrational. Gradually the new concepts won widespread acceptance until today their use in scholarly history to explain human action evokes no surprise. This does not mean that the historical profession has deliberately considered the implications of modern psychology or mastered its findings or applied its techniques. It merely means that as a result of one of the deeply significant developments in knowledge, twentieth-century Americans often thought in the new terms. The anti-intellectualism which found encouragement in the new psychology and the emphasis which some exponents placed on sexual drives and frustrations made the theories distasteful to many who repudiated them by name but used them in practice. Surely one of the noticeable changes in any comparison of histories written at the beginning of the century and at its midpoint is the frequent explanation at the later date of human behavior as lying outside the area of conscious control.

III

When one turns from a consideration of the influence of basic concepts to look at the actual history written and studied by the recently established professional group of scholars, probably the first thing to be noted is the remarkable expansion of activity. Almost every portion of the long story of the human race has been the subject of intensive study by Americans in the twentieth century. Specialists are now available where fifty years ago there was either total ignorance or a bare minimum of knowledge. The list of organizations and journals already given indicates the change. It is true that certain areas such as India, the Balkans, Brazil, or the Byzantine Empire are thinly covered. It is also true that there has been retrogression in some fields. In 1900 a very large percentage of the few historical scholars there were had some knowledge of the history of peoples in the Holy Land in Biblical times. Today though there may be more who could be ranked as specialists, only a minute fraction of the body of scholars has any of this knowledge. In spite of outstanding contributions by twentieth-century American scholars to knowledge of the ancient world there has also been a sufficiently noticeable decline in the undergraduate study of the histories of ancient Greece and Rome to make some observers fear that scholarly knowledge of those momentous periods may atrophy or become the sterile possession of a few learned anchorites. The most distinguished professors of ancient history have, as a group, produced relatively few young scholars to take their places. Indeed there has been a tendency in even the leading universities not to replace professors in ancient history who retire or die. Undoubtedly a partial explanation lies in the fact that there has been a concomitant or earlier decline in the knowledge of the classical languages. Practically every arts college in the United States required some knowledge of Latin for admission in 1900, and some required Greek. Practically no arts college has such a requirement in 1950. A minority of the high schools of the country offer courses in Latin, which are taken by a still smaller minority of the students, and only a rare preparatory school gives instruction in Greek. . . .

If scholarly activity in a few areas contracted relatively or absolutely, there took place a remarkable expansion in other areas. This was particularly true of the study of American history. In 1890 when Herbert B. Adams was being promoted to a professorship in the Johns Hopkins University, after he had made his department the leading one in United States for graduate study, he recorded the contemporary position of American history in his comments about his title. "I have no ambition" wrote his teacher of F. J. Turner, C. M. Andrews, J. Franklin Jameson, and many others noted for scholarly contributions in American history, "to be known as a Professor of American History. At least five sixths of my three years' course of lectures to graduates and *all* of my undergraduate classes are in the European field . . . As 'Professor of Institutional History' I could have a fair field for comparative studies in Church and State and the Institutes of Education, without being regarded as an American provincial."[9] That Adams spoke for his generation can be seen from other evidence. Princeton University in its catalogue for the academic year 1900-1901 also listed no course in American History for its undergraduates. At Harvard in 1899-1900, of the twenty courses in history, including five offered jointly with the Divinity School, only three were on American history. At Yale in the same year the proportion was higher, since three of the eleven courses given were devoted to America. During the next fifty years American history became the most diligently cultivated field of scholarly activity. The Harvard catalogue of 1948-49 showed that eighteen of the fifty undergraduate courses in history, including six given jointly with the Divinity School, were listed as American history. Comparable shifts took place elsewhere and, of course, in the scholarly profession at large. They seem likely to continue if the doctoral dissertations in progress at universities in the United States are a guide to the work of the next generation. A list of dissertations in progress in September 1949, published by the American Historical Association, showed that 894 of a total of 1,634 were on the history of the United States.

In seeking the explanation for the greater emphasis on American history several factors can be readily identified. The relative ease of getting at source materials for American history and the labor involved in acquiring the knowledge of foreign languages essential in most of the other fields of history undoubtedly account in part for the larger number of graduate students in the former. More important has been the intensification of nationalism everywhere and especially, of course, in the United States since the Spanish-American War and since the American people became a self-conscious world

[9] Holt, *Historical Scholarship in the United States*, pp. 145-146.

power. Repeatedly from 1914 to 1950 the American people, speaking through newspapers, through national and state legislatures, and through various other media, have demanded that more American history be taught. American scholars, sharing the same impulses, have not been slow to comply.

Another partial explanation of the emphasis on American history is the much greater attention given to what is called recent history. Between 1900 and 1950 there has been a chronological as well as a geographical expansion of scholarly activity. The most significant extension in time has not been to earlier periods through archaeological or other discoveries. On the contrary, it has resulted from the inclusion of the most recent period within the jurisdiction of scholarship. The shift in emphasis can be measured by contrasting the practice in Justin Winsor's *Narrative and Critical History of America,* which is typical of the preprofessional nineteenth-century scholarship, and *The American Nation* series, which represents the ideas and interests of the twentieth-century scholarly profession. The former shows that the prevailing view considered the terminal point for the scholarly treatment of American history to be the American Revolution and the constitutional convention of 1789, or events of a full century earlier. The latter devoted four of twenty-five volumes to the forty years preceding and including the date of publication. As the twentieth century advanced, the shift of scholarly focus to recent history persisted, until by 1950 a large percentage of the work being done not only in American history but in British, Latin American, Modern European, and Far Eastern history covered the immediately preceding decades, a period which an earlier generation would have regarded as not a proper field for scholarship. The editor of the *American Historical Review* stated in 1915 that in the first twenty years of that journal only eight out of nearly four hundred articles related to the history of Europe since 1815. In 1920 he reported that as a consequence of the new focus of interest produced by the World War a dozen articles on European history after 1815 had been added in the five-year period.[10] The most superficial glance at the courses offered in various institutions, at the tables of contents in scholarly journals, and at the dissertations in progress shows that since 1920 more and more attention has been paid to the recent period in Europe, America, and Asia.

Both the geographical and chronological changes have been reflected in the programs of the annual meeting of the professional organization. In December 1899 the American Historical Association met in Boston. About 150 members, most of whom were not university professors, attended. There were five sessions at which fifteen scholarly papers were read, not counting the presidential address. The subjects at the five sessions were Colonization (in general), Church History, European History, Foreign Relations (chiefly of the United States), and Fields of Historical Study (military, economic, and sacred and profane). In December 1949 the American Historical Association again met in Boston. The number of members who registered was 1,173. Probably well over 90 per cent of them were present or prospective members of the academic world. There were 47 sessions with 204 participants, including chairmen and commentators as well as the authors of the papers. Approximately one-third of the sessions dealt with American history. Others were devoted to the histories of Great Britain, France, Germany, Russia, China, India, Latin-America, of the ancient, medieval, and Renaissance periods, to economic history, to military history, to the history of religion, to the history of science and to the history of education, and to methods and problems in teaching history.

There have been still further changes in scholarly focus

[10] J. Franklin Jameson, "The American Historical Review, 1895-1920," *American Historical Review*, XXVI (October, 1920), 17.

which are worth noting. Within each area and each period the historians burst the bonds which had confined history so largely to the political activities of man. No department of history would in 1950 dream of inscribing on its walls and its publications the motto "History is Past Politics and Politics is Present History" as was done in the 1880's by the preëminent graduate school of that period.[11] Judging by the history written, history has been expanded to include all past human activities. Moreover, laudable if not always successful efforts have been made to achieve a synthesis of man's multifarious exploits. Still some fields of action have received more attention than others, an inevitable result which is magnified by the prevalence of the monograph in scholarly work.

It is, however, true that more political history has been, and still is being, written than any other type. The prevailing strength of nationalism in the United States, as well as in the rest of the world, precluded any possibility of shifting the main focus of attention from the political state. Another explanation for the scholarly emphasis on political history is that in nearly every country and in nearly every period political records have been better preserved and are therefore more easily available than the materials for man's other activities. Perhaps historians themselves by their very interest in the past may be more inclined to follow tradition than other people. Certainly it seems to have been difficult for them to shift their focus from political events. In the Editors' Introduction to *The American Nation* series published in the early years of the twentieth century an emphatic statement announced that the series would not be simply a political or constitutional history but would include as equally important social and economic history. In spite of good intentions and some obvious efforts, the twenty-six volumes which followed represented man as primar-

[11] Herbert B. Adams of the Johns Hopkins University adopted this statement of the English historian, Edward A. Freeman.

ily a political being. Even in the *History of American Life* series, most of which appeared in the fourth decade of the century and which did in fact subordinate political events to economic and social activities, the history of the American people is divided into periods, and the series into volumes by political dates. Sometime there may be a series in which the boundaries of the segments will be the recurring economic crises.

Within the field of political history a number of noteworthy developments occurred. Constitutional history has been relatively neglected and the history of international relations has been greatly emphasized compared to the practice of the nineteenth century. The new position of the United States in world politics after 1898, and the two world wars after periods of severe tension among the world powers, are sufficient to account for the more intensive study of international relations. It is noteworthy that in the histories of foreign relations the more sophisticated scholarly standards that emerged during the period required multiarchival research. Prior to the twentieth century only the exceptional American historian felt the need for data from the records of all the participants in an international dispute. The same scholarly sophistication produced a change in the treatment of the internal political history not only of the United States but of any society. Less consideration has been given to laws and constitutional theory and much more to the actual operation of the political institution. This tendency can be seen by comparing earlier and later accounts of slavery in America and of the British mercantile policy in the colonial period. Military history, because of a combination of circumstances including the reluctance of the liberally minded American scholars to admit that war can be regarded as a normal activity of civilized man, did not share in the popularity of international diplomatic relations. The relative neglect of military history ended, temporarily at least, with World War II. Then the Army, Navy, and Air Force, far surpassing any previous action of the American government, paid tribute to the utility of history by recruiting staffs of historians, most of them in the higher echelons from the scholarly world. The result has been a greatly increased amount of scholarly, though official, military history.

If political history has continued in the twentieth century to be the most common variety, the most startling development was the advent of economic history to a prominence which challenged the supremacy of political history. Whatever the reasons, there can be no doubt that man's activities in producing, distributing, and consuming wealth and the interpretation of his other actions in the light of these operations assumed a new and huge importance in the thought and work of historical scholars during the twentieth century. The earlier writers had not been unaware of human toil but generally either dismissed it as unworthy of attention or treated it in terms of the laws, the policies, the restraints, or aids with which political society attempted to control economic events. It was only in the present century that the canvas supplanted the frame, that economic facts became an end in themselves. The program of the new self-conscious economic historians has been well stated by one of them:

> We are trying to see the farmer farming, rather than watching him go to granger meetings, embark on populist crusades, clamor for greenbacks, or lobby for more than a hundred per cent of parity. We are realizing that the history of labor is not fully or even largely told by narrating the history of labor unions or socialist movements, that the history of banking is more than an account of banking or currency laws, that trade is more than a matter of tariffs, and that even the history of business itself can be studied in terms of the accumulation of capital, the organization and administration of the enterprise, and the development of policies of production of sale.[12]

[12] Herbert Heaton, "The Economic Impact on History," in J. R. Strayer (ed.), *The Interpretation of History* (Princeton, N.J.: Princeton University Press, 1943), pp. 111-112. See also his "Recent Developments in Economic History," *American Historical Review,* XLVII (July, 1942), 727-746.

Fired with the zeal of explorers in a new country, the same professional motives affecting all the scholars, the economic historians quickly won recognition for their field and themselves. They naturally formed their own organization, the Economic History Association, and established a scholarly journal, the *Journal of Economic History,* which is, however, only one of a number of scholarly journals devoted to economic history. Their accomplishments have been considerable in all areas and periods of history. Among them are such monuments as the works of Rostovtzeff and of Tenney Frank on the economic history of the ancient world, the studies of a group of scholars on price fluctuations in western Europe, the volumes on American manufacturing, labor, and agriculture published in a series by the Carnegie Institution of Washington, the Harvard Studies in Business History, and many others too numerous even to list, as well as a veritable flood of monographs.

Political and economic history absorbed most but by no means all of the time and energy of the scholars of the new century. An increasing amount of attention was devoted to other human activities, to thought, to amusements, to eating, to science, to religion, all frequently thrown together under the label "Social History." Whether or not social history constituted "The New History," as was claimed and denied, and whether or not the emphasis placed by some social historians on what the common man ate and wore and did tended "to reduce the chronicle of human striving to its lowest common denominator," as at least one critic asserted, there can be no doubt of its increasing popularity in scholarly circles.[13] This is

---

[13] The classic statement of *The New History* is the book with that title by James Harvey Robinson which was published in 1912. Caustic and penetrating criticisms are in Wilbur Cortez Abbott, "Some 'New' History and Historians," *Proceedings of the Massachusetts Historical Society,* LXIV (1931), 3-35, and Crane Brinton, "The New History: Twenty-five Years Later," *Journal of Social Philosophy,* I (January, 1936), 134-147.

true in spite of the obvious difficulties in trying to relate these disparate aspects of life or to achieve a synthesis of them. The most noteworthy achievements were those in the history of thought and science. Many of the very significant studies in the history of thought were made by professors of literature. The history of science won widespread recognition as a distinct field of specialization to which professors of philosophy contributed more frequently than scientists and as frequently as the scholars located in departments of history.

No matter what the period treated, or the area or the activity, the data must be interpreted according to some scheme of reference if the result is not be be a mere compilation of facts. In seeking the schools of historical interpretation which dominated the work of the scholars in twentieth-century America several facts stand out. The first is that in general the Americans did not subscribe to any single school of historical interpretation. A second fact is that a few years before the beginning of the century there appeared the two most distinctive and original interpretations of history yet formulated by any American scholar. Of these one had no perceptible influence on scholarship. The other founded a school of historical writing which gave its author a greater influence on American historical scholarship than that exerted by any other one man.

In 1890 there had appeared *The Influence of Sea Power upon History, 1660-1783* by Alfred Thayer Mahan, then a Captain in the United States Navy. The thesis in it and in subsequent volumes appearing within a decade was that sea power determined supremacy in international affairs. This hypothesis and the supporting histories won him various high scholarly distinctions, and such influence on the naval policies of the great powers that when he died, the resolution of the American Historical Association recording his death stated that "more than any American scholar of his day he has affected the course of world politics."[14] The times, so propitious for his influence on governmental policy, were decidedly inauspicious for any influence on American historical scholarship. In fact he cannot be said to have had any discernible effect at all.

Instead of being illustrated in many volumes of his own, the thesis of Frederick Jackson Turner reached the scholarly world through an essay published in 1893. Its title, "The Significance of the Frontier in American History," indicated his belief that American history was shaped by the ever westward expanding frontier. It would be difficult to exaggerate the extent or the magnitude of the impact of Turner's interpretation on American historical scholarship. With extraordinary speed the thesis was applied to episode after episode in American history by more and more of the expanding number of scholars. The most distinctly American school of historical interpretation thus became a prominent feature of the twentieth century. There were many explanations for the unparalleled success of the thesis. The most obvious was its validity, its usefulness in bringing light and understanding. Other factors which contributed were the reaction against previous historical ideas, many of them German in origin; the appeal of the uniqueness of American history because of our frontier; the stress on what were considered highly desirable and typically American qualities such as individualism and democracy; the readiness of scholars to accept Darwinian or evolutionary ideas; and the ease with which scattered scholars could study the frontier in their own vicinity.

If such a concatenation of circumstances favored Turner's thesis, time would certainly bring changes. So it proved. After a generation of its unchallenged ascendancy, some

[14] *Annual Report of the American Historical Association for the Year 1914*, I, 53.

scholars began to attack the frontier interpretation, or at least to demand serious modifications of it. The resulting scholarly discussion has produced a literature of its own, and though Turner remains a giant in American historiography, some of his conclusions and more of those put forward by enthusiastic disciples must be abandoned or altered.

There was another interpretation of history used in twentieth-century America even more than the Turner thesis, which in some respects could be regarded as similar. This was the economic interpretation of history. In no sense original with Americans, nor confined to the twentieth century, the explanation of events in terms of economic forces and motives became more widely used among American scholars than any other interpretation. There have been very few American scholars who have employed a strict Marxian economic determinism. Yet if little has been heard of the class struggle, there have been many who have relied chiefly on an economic interpretation and only a rare exception has failed to take some cognizance of the theory. The first startling and successful application of this school to American history was Charles A. Beard's *An Economic Interpretation of the Constitution* which appeared in 1913. From then on, economic interpretation flourished like the proverbial green bay tree, until toward the middle of the century more and more scholars repudiated it as a single explanation and insisted other forces and factors must also be taken into account.

Two other schools of historical interpretation deserve notice. One has been firmly established by extensive work, the other is barely in the process of emerging. The first has properly been called "The Imperial School of Colonial History." Either because of greater scholarly sophistication, or because the outcome of the Spanish-American War made Americans appreciate what had been missed before, or because of both, a new interpretation of the colonial period began in

America around the turn of the century. The colonial period, including the Revolution, was viewed from the center of the empire instead of from the periphery, as a part of British history rather than as the origins of the United States. Since many of the younger generation of scholars were trained in the first decades of the century by men engaged in research in the colonial period this school had a wide influence, and its finest products, represented by the histories of Beer, Osgood, Andrews, and Gipson, compared favorably with the best scholarship of the period.[15]

The other interpretation cannot be said to have been formulated as a fully developed thesis. Yet it is evident that in the latter part of the half-century a number of scholars began to regard the urban movement as decisive a factor in all phases of post Civil War American history as the frontier and westward movement had been earlier. Professor A. M. Schlesinger, whose article in 1940 contains the nearest approach so far to a statement of the new thesis, has also made in *The Rise of the City, 1878-1898*, the most notable, if not entirely successful, attempt to use the urban movement as the synthesizing agency in recent American history.[16] What the ultimate result will be is still an open question but one to which an answer may soon be given.

---

[15] There is a chapter on "The Imperial School of Colonial History" in Michael Kraus, *A History of American History* (New York: Farrar and Rinehart, Inc., 1937). See also, Lawrence H. Gipson, "Charles McLean Andrews and the Re-orientation of the Study of American Colonial History," *Pennsylvania Magazine of History and Biography*, LIX (July, 1935), 209-222, and Max Savelle, "The Imperial School of American Colonial Historians," *Indiana Magazine of History*, XLV (June, 1949), 123-134.

[16] Arthur M. Schlesinger, "The City in American History," *Mississippi Valley Historical Review*, XXVII (June, 1940), 43-66. The book, published in 1933, is Volume X of *A History of American Life* edited by Schlesinger and Dixon Ryan Fox. See also, William Diamond, "On the Dangers of an Urban Interpretation," in Eric F. Goldman (ed.), *Historiography and Urbanization* (Baltimore, Md.: The Johns Hopkins Press, 1941).

This answer, together with all the answers to the problems confronting historical scholarship in America in the middle of the twentieth century, will depend on the wisdom as well as the learning of the members of the history departments of the universities and colleges. No analysis of the study and writing of history in twentieth-century America can exaggerate the part played by this professional group. Nor can one fail to pay tribute to the high scholarly standards which they employed in making their remarkable additions to knowledge and understanding.

Yet significant as have been the scholarly benefits resulting from the appearance in America of a class of professional historians, the transfer of historical scholarship so exclusively to their hands may in the end prove to have been unfortunate. History is concerned with life, and he who wishes to understand or interpret human activity must himself have participated in affairs and the richer his experience the better. That is what Gibbon meant when, referring to his own brief military career, he said the Captain of the Hampshire Grenadiers was of use to the historian of Rome. That is what ex-Senator Foraker of Ohio meant when he wrote in 1911 to a friend explaining his objections to William Howard Taft and Theodore Roosevelt. Neither, he said, has "ever earned a dollar except by earning a salary or writing a magazine article or in some such way. Neither one ever had any business experience. Neither ever knew what it was to meet a pay roll Saturday night—or to wrestle with a deficit."[17] This type of criticism may be applied with equal validity to the writing of history. There is always danger that the professional historians may spend too much of their lives in libraries. It is probably fortunate that so many of the group during World War I and World

[17] Gibbon's comment is, of course, in his famous autobiography. That of Senator Foraker was in a letter to A. W. Jones, December 9, 1911. MSS. Foraker Papers, Library of Congress.

War II participated directly in military and other public service. Scholarly training and much learning are not adequate substitutes for experience. They can produce technicians but not the rich, wise minds from which alone great history can be expected.

Who Reads the Best Histories?

USUALLY I TAKE a dim view of the scholarly value of selections of the best presidents, of the best secretaries of state, or of the best anything. Of course I read all such lists avidly and compare them to their disadvantage with the list I would have prepared. But I always doubt the value of them for any purpose other than amusement. The list which Professor Caughey assembled and which has surely been carefully scrutinized and much discussed in academic circles is a different order of being. A few more than one hundred scholars indicated the books which they considered to be the best histories and biographies published during the past thirty years. The resulting consensus is thus a composite book review, and book reviews have a significant role to play. The reviewer is the custodian of our scholarly standards and his defense of them will determine the quality of the books which will be written.

The list is valuable in other ways. An analysis of it reveals many facts that should be pondered by the students and writers of history in America. Some of these have been pointed out by Professor Caughey in the text accompanying the list. One of his statements was particularly challenging and has furnished the aspect of the problem which I have investigated. He wrote: "Sometimes it is asserted that history to be popular has to be watered down, dramatized, over-written, or otherwise distorted. That the historians in this poll put their seal of approval on so many books that were best sellers or near best sellers is encouraging. It suggests that the great books in American history, at least a good many of them, sold well and are generally available to be read."

This optimistic statement concerns a vitally important problem. Is the best history, or even ordinary scholarly history, read by anyone? Is it by specialists for specialists? Does the knowledge reach *the* public, or *a* public? Many of us have reflected on this serious subject. Recently my own thoughts went like this: Scholarly history in the twentieth century was not read by the public to the same extent as the scholarly history of earlier periods. This fact did not disturb scholars in the early years of the century. Indeed they saw in it cause for satisfaction. In their desire to be scientific and in their aversion to predecessors whom they scornfully labeled "literary historians," they deliberately shunned a felicitous literary style which might encourage reading by the public. The cold and unadorned style of a laboratory report fitted more closely their theory of history as science. Naturally the public being under no professional compulsion to read the monographs or journals did not do so.

One fact must be recorded to the credit of the historical scholars. They have at no time created and used a specialized or technical terminology. In thus refusing to follow the example of scholars in most branches of knowledge, including economics, sociology, psychology, philosophy, and education, to mention only a few, the historians denied themselves some advantages. The general public, as well as colleagues in the academic world, could not be impressed by an awesome vocabulary, incomprehensible to all save the initiated. More importantly, the historians, lacking specially designed words, have employed those commonly used and hence often loosely used. Words like "cause" and "fact" have, in fact, caused a lot of trouble. Offsetting these disadvantages is the one great gain. If the historians have anything of moment to say and if they can say it with even a modicum of literary art, the public will be able to understand it. Admittedly, the scholars in history at the beginning of the century were not taking advantage of this opportunity and were out of touch with the reading public.

Gradually during the twentieth century the profession became dissatisfied with this situation against which there had always been a few protestants. The cause of the change in attitude was neither a desire for royalties nor pressure from commercial publishers, since the latter willingly left the publication of historical monographs to the rapidly expanding university presses. To some extent the scholars began to take less seriously the theory of history as science, a theory which tended to make history dull. Greater weight can be attributed to World War I which stimulated nationalism and which confronted the historical profession, some through direct personal experience, with the problem of making historical knowledge more directly useful to the American people. One conclusion quickly reached was that scholarly knowledge had been kept too largely within the small circle of scholars. The obvious remedy was to write scholarly history in a way that the public would read. In the second quarter of the century the new attitude won general acceptance and more and more of the monographic work came to be written if not with literary art at least with greater effectiveness than before.

Thus I pointed at much the same optimistic conclusion which Professor Caughey stated more positively in the words I have already quoted. His list suggested a test and, forgetting the wisdom of the man who warned against measuring a happy thought, I proceeded to collect facts. First I selected twenty of the sixty best histories and biographies. My selection was a random one except that I eliminated books that have been used as textbooks, like Beard's *Rise of American Civilization* and Morison and Commager's *Growth of the American Republic,* and books that were by men outside the academic world like Charles Warren, Van Wyck Brooks, Carl Sandburg, Douglas Freeman, Robert Sherwood, and others. Eight of my twenty selections were biographies; the other twelve were histories, seven from the years 1920 to 1935 and five from the years 1935 to 1950. Then I wrote to the publishers and asked for figures on sales. Although publishers are naturally reluctant to reveal their sales to competitors they responded generously when I explained the purpose for which I was requesting the data. Here is what I found.

Six of the twenty works sold over 10,000 copies; those at the top of the list being aided by the fact that one or another of the various book clubs included them in its offerings. Two of the six, as well as three others among the twenty, were awarded the Pulitzer Prize, a fact which should have stimulated sales among the public if not within scholarly circles. The six were:

Admiral of the Ocean Sea, by Samuel E. Morison, 2 vols., 1942   18,200
(Of the one-volume edition, plus the entire two-volume edition of unknown size.)

The American Mind, by Henry S. Commager, 1950   17,631

Jefferson and His Time, by Dumas Malone, 2 vols., 1948-1951   13,483
(Of Volume I only; Volume II was published after 1950.)

Life and Labor in the Old South, by Ulrich B. Phillips, 1929   12,290

History of the United States, by Edward Channing, 6   11,511
   vols., 1905-1925
   (Ranging from 14,400 of Volume I to 8,600 of
   Volume VI.)[1]

Maritime History of Massachusetts, by Samuel E.
   Morison   10,800

Then came four books with sales between five and ten
thousand. They were:

Edmund Ruffin, by Avery O. Craven, 1931   9,079
The Declaration of Independence, by Carl Becker,   7,600
   1922
   (This book was published in 1922 and the first edition of "something less than 3,000 copies" went out
   of print in 1927. A publisher who reprints scholarly
   books re-issued an edition of 500 copies in 1933 and
   sold the last "a few months" before September, 1953.
   A third publisher re-issued the book in 1942 and sold
   approximately 4,100 copies by September, 1953.)

The Colonial Period of American History, by Charles
   M. Andrews, 4 vols., 1934-1938   6,442
   (Ranging from 7,925 of Volume I to 5,321 of
   Volume III.)

Hamilton Fish, by Allan Nevins, 1935   about 5,000

The next group clustered around the figure of three thousand. There were also four in it:

The Atlantic Migration, by Marcus L. Hansen, 1940   3,900
   (An unknown quantity is still unsold.)

Thorstein Veblen and His America, by Joseph Dorf-
   man, 1934   3,609

The Sod-House Frontier, by Everett N. Dick, 1938   3,165

Henry Clay, by Bernard Mayo, 1937   2,950

---

[1] The figures on the sale of Channing were taken from John A. De Novo, "Edward Channing's 'Great Work' Twenty Years After," *Mississippi Valley Historical Review*, XXXIX (September, 1952), 274.

Then came four works with sales of under fifteen hundred. These were:

The Populist Revolt, by John D. Hicks, 1931   1,500
(This work went out of print in 1948.)

The American Revolution Considered as a Social Movement, by J. Franklin Jameson, 1926   1,356
(The first publisher, a university press, sold 956 copies. A second publisher twenty-four years later, or in 1950, re-issued an edition of 400 copies. It went out of stock in 1953.)

John Jacob Astor, by Kenneth W. Porter, 2 vols., 1931   1,115

The British Empire before the American Revolution, by Lawrence H. Gipson, 7 vols., 1936-1949   915
(Average for the last four volumes; the average for the entire seven is not over 950.)

In two cases the publishers refused to give figures. One stated that there was one large printing, whatever that may mean, of Craven's *Coming of the Civil War* in 1942 and that it is "enjoying a steady annual sale." The other reported that Vann Woodward's *Tom Watson* is out of print after "a fair but hardly substantial sale while it was available."

Let me summarize these results by pointing out that eight of the eighteen best books for which I have more or less exact figures sold fewer than four thousand copies. To appreciate the significance of that statement a few more statistics are necessary. I will refrain from mentioning the population of the United States and the sales of books like *The Power of Positive Thinking,* or *A Man Called Peter,* or *Tallulah.* Neither will I cite the sales of Parkman, Motley, or Bancroft, although they might well provoke thought.[2] I will refer only to

[2] I cannot refrain from mentioning that Prescott's first history, *Ferdinand and Isabella,* published at his own expense, sold out an edition of 1,250 in five weeks, and that Motley's first historical work, also published at his own expense because no publisher would assume the risk, sold 15,000 copies in two years. This was in a period when the population of the United States was only a small fraction of its present total.

statistics bearing on the learned population in the United States. According to the nineteenth edition of *The American Library Directory,* published in 1951, there were 11,034 libraries in the United States. The 6,416 public libraries, not counting branches, should, one would think, buy some of these histories and biographies. But let us ignore them for the libraries concerned solely with higher education. There were 1,425 college and university libraries as well as 558 junior college libraries, a total of 1,983, or slightly larger than the number of accredited institutions of higher learning published by the Federal Office of Education. To this potential market must be added the professors of American history. I know of no figures on them. My estimate is that there are about 7,500 faculty members teaching history in institutions of higher learning and my guess is that between one third and one half of them teach American history, the proportion being larger in the smaller colleges.

You have undoubtedly already correlated some of the data I have submitted to you. Even if not a single copy had been sold to a single member of the general public or to a single public library, and of course some were, the total number of Hicks's *The Populist Revolt* sold was not enough to supply each college and university library, not to mention the professors of American history. Jameson's *American Revolution Considered as a Social Movement,* with a total sale of 1,356 copies, is available to only a small proportion of the people concerned with giving or receiving higher education. Young students at the majority of our colleges can obtain the benefit of that scholarly work only in diluted form through a textbook or through the lectures of a professor if he read it when doing graduate work at one of the larger universities. The case of Gipson's magnificent work on *The British Empire before the American Revolution,* which received the second highest number of votes among the more recent histories, shocked me even more than that of Jameson's book, which at least sold out the small edition printed by a university press. The firm which publishes Gipson's work cannot be held responsible for the tragically small sales, since it has as good a record generally as any of the publishers currently operating. Indeed we who are interested in scholarship owe it a deep debt of gratitude because the publication of this large work is, as stated in their letter to me, "a labor of love" which has been done "at a very, very considerable loss."

These statistics raise serious questions about the book-buying habits of both the professor and the college and university libraries.[3] Remember that these twenty books are among the sixty selected as the best of the last thirty years by a jury of over one hundred scholars. Remember also that many of the larger universities have ten or more copies of these books. In addition, an unknown but probably significant number have been sold to the general public and to public libraries. Note that it took seventeen years to sell 1,500 copies of Hicks's *The Populist Revolt;* that after Jameson's *The American Revolution Considered as a Social Movement* had been cited in all textbooks and monographs for a generation, only 400 copies were sold in three years when a publisher risked a re-issue; and that after the first edition of fewer than 3,000 copies of Becker's *The Declaration of Independence* was exhausted in 1927, a new issue of 500 copies, which was the only edition available for the nine years from 1933 to 1942, was not sold

[3] Perhaps the Mississippi Valley Historical Association should canvass its members to see how many of the sixty books are in the possession of each member. I happen to own eleven of the thirty titles in history and fourteen of the thirty biographies. It would interest me to know how I rate in relation to other members of the profession in this respect. I find on checking that I have one more of the sixty books than the fourth largest university in the State of Washington, which with an enrollment of about 1,500 students has twenty-four of the sixty. The University of Washington Library has 59, the Seattle Public Library 58, and the Tacoma Public Library 52.

out until 1953. One cannot help but wonder who orders the books purchased by our college and university libraries. A second matter of speculation concerns the number and quality of the scholarly books the members of the profession purchase for themselves.

Certainly the figures on sales prove that the effort at reaching the public, which I described in print as a feature of the second quarter of the century, has so far met with complete failure. Certainly, also, they are hard to reconcile with Professor Caughey's statement that "great books in American history, at least a good many of them, sold well and are generally available to be read." Indeed they force me to the disturbing conclusion that most of our scholarly history, including the best, is not by specialists for specialists but is by specialists for a small fraction of the specialists.

History and the Social Sciences Reconsidered

OF THE ENTIRE human species, and especially of those who concern themselves with knowledge and scholarship, we who study, teach and write history are the most colossally impudent. The physicist seeks only to know and understand the inanimate world of matter. The economist confines his investigations to that fictitious fraction known as the economic man who does nothing but produce and distribute wealth, or in words of the report, the economist develops his subject by abstracting particular patterns from the general complex of human behavior. The psychologist is concerned with another fragment of man, starting or ending with mental or emotional activities but covering many others in the process. So it is with all the many specialists who have emerged with bewildering rapidity during the past century when accumulated knowledge has reached vast and complex proportions. The cultural anthropologist is not overmodest in setting boundaries to his field of knowledge, but compared to us in history he is a shrinking violet. The historian alone has the effrontery to assert that it is his task to synthesize all knowledge and to tell the complete story of man in all his activities and aspects, including his relations with the material world. It is true that economists, psychologists and all the rest, recognizing the inadequacy of their partial accounts, frequently wander far afield to offer more satisfactory explanations than the limitations of their subjects permit. Indeed just as the physicist and the chemist who push their studies to the present frontiers of knowledge, find their subjects blending, so also do the various specialists in the social sciences. But the historian alone proclaims it as his primary duty and responsibility to seek and tell the whole truth. To cap this climax the historian normally expects to do all the necessary original research.

Far from rejecting this presumptuous conception of the role of the historian, I believe it to be precisely correct. The human mind being what it is someone has to attempt the total synthesis and who is better qualified to do so, or perhaps I should say should be better qualified to do so, than the historian.

These thoughts lead me to my first comment on the report of the Committee on Historiography. It is a comment not a criticism, yet a comment that needs to be made in order to place the report in its proper perspective. Unlike the previous report, no. 54,[1] which was concerned with the problems and the fundamental presuppositions of history in its all-inclusive sense, this report treats only of the relations of history with the social sciences or, as the title of the semi-final draft of the report put it, "The Social Science Approach to History." True, the so-called social sciences probably contain the most fruitful and significant knowledge for the historian, and certainly the Committee is justified in restricting their study to a partial approach to history, especially since they label it as such. Yet a reminder that the social science historian is a

---

[1] *Theory and Practise in Historical Study: A Report of the Committee on Historiography* (New York: Social Science Research Council, Bulletin 54, 1946), xi + 177 pp.

lesser being than the historian may be in order. Social science history, like patriotism, is not enough. Although the Committee is aware of this there are places in the report which read as if they had temporarily forgotten it and as if they believed that the social science approach would lead to the complete answer, to the total synthesis.

A more serious matter is the failure, or so it seems to me, to make clear just what the social science approach to history is. By "the social science approach" the Committee does not refer to the facts or knowledge in the various social sciences which the historian can take and use. They mean the procedure which is employed in the social sciences to arrive at understanding and truth. The procedure involves the deliberate use of theory, concept, hypothesis, or what is called "an operational working hypothesis," cumulative analysis and other steps in rational operations. Of the merits and desirability of such a method in studying and writing history I have no doubts. Indeed in a small way I recently attempted to apply that very procedure to a historical problem that interested me. What I do object to is the assertion that this method is a social science approach. To the best of my exceedingly limited understanding of such matters this method or procedure is also that of the physical or so-called exact sciences, indeed these may have a prior or better claim to the method. For this belief I find support in some of the books the Committee itself uses to describe the method. Bridgman's *The Logic of Modern Physics* and Conant's *On Understanding Science* are prominently cited to illustrate or explain the very method which is being described as distinctive of the social sciences. Let me repeat I am not objecting to the method, which I believe should be and could profitably be employed by historians. Only I believe it to be scientific method, not social science method. In consequence, when I look for what is meant by the social science approach I do not find an answer that convinces me there is a separate social science procedure or method. This, I submit, is more than a quibble about words.

If we admit, as we must, that the historian should be informed of the concepts and hypotheses by which the non-historical social sciences develop and that he should also be able to incorporate in his synthesis the latest findings of the social sciences, we can readily agree with the Committee that the historian's task is one of considerably greater complexity than that which faces any single one of the non-historical social sciences. How difficult and complex it is can be illustrated by the experiences of the Committee when they tried to assemble a brief summary of the social science theories or hypotheses which might be of special use to the historian. They requested one or more specialists in each science to prepare a paper on the value of the concepts and theories of his particular discipline for historical purposes. Each of these papers was then discussed at length. The desired result was not attained. In the words of one draft of the report "no chains of empirically testable propositions that might be called a coherent theory emerged from any of the discussions" and the proposed chapter became "a kind of dictionary of useful terms and concepts." Even this had to be abandoned because it was found that the various social scientists could not agree on the definitions of the terms and concepts. Consequently, the Committee limited itself to a survey of the social sciences, pointing out the most promising areas of development and the areas of most interest to the historian.

This survey which constitutes the longest chapter in the report is, I believe, a remarkable *tour de force*. I found the accounts of recent trends and achievements in the various social sciences stimulating, enlightening and profitable. I have a strong suspicion that some specialists in the several fields might disagree, perhaps even vigorously, with the statements of the objectives and current status of their science. Certainly those geographers who concentrate on human geography may register objection to being omitted completely from the social sciences. Still for me and any other historians who have found themselves unable to keep abreast of the rapidly growing social sciences this survey has genuine value. We will not care if the necessarily brief accounts are too dogmatic or not hedged with sufficient qualifications.

One feature of the survey, and for that matter of the entire report, which will give us pause, is the presence of a large number of technical and abstract terms, the meanings of which we must learn. Obviously, the historian must understand the language employed in the separate social sciences if he is to benefit from the specialized knowledge being accumulated. The Committee assumes that if a scholar from another discipline has a general idea of the methods and interests of a particular field, he can, when faced with a research problem, acquire the appropriate knowledge. This assumption is false. The experience of the Committee itself, when it discovered that the social scientists on the Council could not agree on definitions of terms, should have indicated the seriousness of the problem for the historian when he must master specialized languages in which the same term may have different meanings. Moreover, the historian, if he is to meet his responsibility, must be able to translate the technical terms into a common speech which can be understood by the members of all the social sciences and by the general public as well. One of the criticisms which can justly be made against the report is that not enough translation has been done. Most historians will find it necessary, as I did, to shed much mental sweat before they can feel that they really understand the technical terms with which the report abounds.

What makes the burden still heavier is that one of the languages now regularly employed in some of the social sciences is mathematics, and mathematics on a higher level than that normally reached by historians. Does this mean we must spend even more years in preparation before we can do our work in history? And is there not danger as well as absurdity in the situation? If he knows not England who only England knows, it is also true that he knows not England who spends his entire life studying India, Australia, France, and Germany to the neglect of England. By the time the would-be historian acquires the knowledge and understanding made possible by psychology, sociology, economics and all the rest, will any time be left to do the necessary research in the records of the past and to compose the total synthesis? Perhaps the answer can be found in the remark of a colleague of mine in economics to whom I took an article in the *American Economic Review* with a request that he tell me what it meant. The article contained a few ordinary words and many mathematical symbols which were manipulated in a series of pleasing designs. My economist friend, a full professor, admitted at once that he too could understand none of it. Nor, he assured me, could the large majority of the professors in economics in the country. When I made the obvious and pointed remarks that we make when finding a colleague as ignorant in his field as we are in our own, he replied that there was no reason to worry, that if new knowledge or light was obtained by the application of complex mathematics there would be some economists able and willing to translate the results into language they all could understand.

Whatever the solution of this part of the large problem, there can be no doubt that the historian, or for that matter any social scientist or any scholar who is applying the findings or techniques of a highly developed branch of knowledge in another field should be certain of their knowledge and of its application. The Committee in the report warns of the damage that can be done by a little knowledge of another field even in so closely related subjects as the social sciences, but in my opinion, does not sufficiently stress the danger. Current scholarly literature offers ample proof of it. Freudian psychology has cast much light on human motives and action, but we have all seen horrible examples of the applications of its terms and of what is thought to be its findings by scholars whose acquaintance with the subject is, to adopt British understatement, slight. Sometimes the question is not the author's mastery of the subject but the deeper issue of whether or not the methods and conclusions of one field of knowledge can be fruitfully or justifiably applied in another field. Let me illustrate. About ten years ago a professor of sociology wrote a large book entitled *Dimensions of Society, A Quantitative Systematics for the Social Sciences.* He belongs to that group of sociologists—to the honor of sociology it should be stated that it is a minority group—who believe that everything, including the love between a man and a woman, can be accurately measured, and stated in a mathematical formula. Because there is such a school of thought the book was taken very seriously and in the same number of the *American Sociological Review* received two lengthy reviews, one by a distinguished sociologist at Harvard, the other by a distinguished mathematician at the California Institute of Technology. The latter replied directly to a fundamental question the author raised when he asked: "Can dimensional analysis of societal situations be used, as dimensional analysis is used in Physics?" The mathematician replied that as a mathematician he would say no, "at least until someone can give a meaningful answer to such exactly analogous questions as 'How many yards of buttermilk does it take to make a pair of britches for a bull?' "[2] There is wisdom as well as amusement in that answer.

[2] The mathematician was E. T. Bell. The review is in the *American Sociological Review,* VII (October, 1942), 707-709. The quotation is on p. 709.

The most valuable section of the report, in my opinion, is the final chapter which discusses some of the studies that should result from an application of the social science approach to history. Probably this appeals because unlike most of the report it shifts from abstract ideas to specific problems to be investigated. Most of us in the field of history feel secure and at ease only when dealing with specific and concrete facts and ideas. Many more illustrations in the other portions of the report would have added greatly to its effectiveness. Exhortations to ascertain the best knowledge in other branches of learning and theoretical descriptions of method in abstract terms are apt to have little impact on the practice of historical writing.

Even in this final chapter when the discussion is focused on illustrations in American history, I would have liked more specific help. It is all very well to state that the changing character of family relations must be studied and used in the historical synthesis since familial conditioning is of fundamental importance in shaping the course of civilization. To that I agree. In fact I have said in print that one of the most significant consequences of the phenomenal drop in the birth rate from the 1880's to the 1930's is the novel psychological experience of Americans who grew to maturity in the period of the low birth rate.[3] The difference between a childhood in a family where there are five or more children and one in a family containing one or no brother or sister must be great. When the one or two child family became typical for so large a proportion of the population it would seem inevitable that changes in behavior and attitudes would be noticeable. Modern psychology can tell us something of the effect on the individual. But the historian who wishes to trace the effects of

[3] Some Consequences of the Urban Movement in American History," *Pacific Historical Review*, **XXII** (November, 1953), p. 344; reprinted in this volume.

the psychology of the small family on the social history of the United States will get no help from this report. The Committee asserts that studies of this sort are precisely those which need to be done, yet offers no suggestions as to where to find materials or how to proceed except by hypothesis and verification.

Another subject for further exploration is one on which I have often speculated. For years I have been telling my classes that we have become a nation of employees, of hired hands, and that the consequences of that fact must be highly important. The statistics on the disappearance of the independent grocer and the substitution for him of a clerk are easy to find, and even the large number of the professions who are now employees of corporations can be estimated. It is not that aspect of the phenomenon which interests me but the psychological effect and the consequent influence on our entire history. Are the American people now dominated by an employee psychology, and, if so, what in our history can be explained by that fact? I regularly confess to the class I do not know, but I am certain much could be explained if I did know. Let me put it this way. The report of the Committee says (p. 163) that "the American people in the early 1930's, facing a new cultural situation, displayed qualities of resignation not easily explicable on the basis of either the traditional or immediate events of their past." Suppose I follow the method advocated so strongly in this report, and deliberately formulate a hypothesis, to wit: The American people displayed these qualities of resignation because the employee psychology and attitudes had become dominant. What then, how do I verify it, what materials can I use, where can I turn? At this point the Committee has nothing to offer.

One other suggestion for further exploration is a repetition of what I said when Report no. 54 appeared. In the modern period scholars are confronted with more source materials than can be read in a life time. The old standard of scholarship requiring an examination of all source materials and of all secondary writings is absurd. Sampling is essential. Some Committee would render historical scholarship a great service by a realistic study of what can and should be done. The complexities of this are vast, the need urgent.

My final comment may appear to be heresy to the members of the Committee and the many who share their approach. Much as I agree with their fundamental position, and certain as I am that understanding and fruitful results can be obtained by the methods the Committee advocates, I apprehend a great disservice to history which may result from an abuse or a too narrow application of their approach. In other words I fear that "the social science" approach may dehumanize mankind. After objecting strongly to the synthesis built around great men and events, and to the prevailing tendency for a popular dramatic frame of reference, the report says (p. 160): "This general approach is often valid when applied to the actions of a single individual, but neither narrative nor popular drama is usually suited to the analysis of mass phenomena. While drama will still be found in the conflict and resolution of forces or in group challenge and response, this is likely to be drama on a nonpopular abstract level." In this attitude I fear I can see the seed which could flourish into a monstrosity comparable to that produced by the sociologists who try to measure emotion in a mathematical formula. I do not subscribe to the great man theory of history. At the same time I object to seeing great men or all the little men reduced to a decimal point of "mass phenomena" in a "drama on a nonpopular abstract level." There is poetry in life. And the history, or any science, that omits the poetry from life is both untrue and dangerous.

An Evaluation of the Report

on Theory and Practice

in Historical Study

SOME YEARS AGO Charles A. Beard stated that even "scholars who devote a lifetime to the critical analysis of historical sources frequently write huge works on history without ever asking themselves just what they are doing."[1] Beard, who spent a large part of his life in the study of sources, and wrote some large and influential works of history, devoted much time in recent years not only to asking that question but to formulating answers to it. Many American scholars who have written and taught history in the past several decades have joined him in the belief that, if the historians were fully aware of what they were doing, of their controlling assumptions, and of the limitations of their methods, their writing of history would be better.

In due course, the historical profession, through the agency of the Social Science Research Council, attempted to clarify thinking about certain historiographical problems. A Com-

[1] Charles A. Beard, *The Discussion of Human Affairs* (New York, 1936), p. 82.

mittee on Historiography was established, composed of eight scholars widely and favorably known in the profession. They were, in addition to Beard, Shepard B. Clough of Columbia University, Thomas C. Cochran of New York University, Louis Gottschalk of the University of Chicago, Jeannette Nichols of Pennsylvania, Alfred Vagts of the Institute for Advanced Study, and Merle Curti of the University of Wisconsin as chairman. The committee decided, in the words of its chairman, that "it could best fulfill its obligations . . . to the historical profession by preparing a manual designed to help clarify thought about history and to aid historians in teaching and writing it."[2]

The expectations naturally aroused when such a group of scholars avow such a purpose are not fulfilled. Their report, it is to be hoped, will provoke and will sometimes clarify thought about the writing and study of history. It will not, however, lead to the desired higher standards of scholarship in the historical profession unless much more work is done. Where the report succeeds in clarifying thought, earlier and equally useful studies were already available. Where the report fails is precisely where, courageously and for the first time in the literature of American historical scholarship, it attempts to formulate the fundamental propositions upon which history as a branch of knowledge rests.

The first chapter, written by Charles A. Beard, is entitled "Grounds for a Reconsideration of Historiography." This chapter could have been omitted without much loss. The rest of the book is more successful in making clear the reasons for the reconsideration of historiography, the nature of some of the problems involved, and the importance of awareness on the part of historians of their own intellectual processes.

[2] *Theory and Practice in Historical Study: A Report of the Committee on Historiography* (New York: Social Science Research Council, Bulletin 54, 1946), p. vii.

The second chapter, "Controlling Assumptions in the Practice of American Historians," is by John Herman Randall, Jr., and George Haines IV. It is a valuable and thoughtful discussion of the part played by the frames of reference according to which historians select certain facts as significant. It examines particularly certain assumptions which have determined the nature of much of the history written in America. The main objection that can be made to this penetrating analysis is that the authors, like good historians, concern themselves too much with past assumptions and too little with those which control the scholars now at work. The present generation can see clearly and can scarcely refrain from smiling at the assumptions of their scholarly grandparents without being keenly aware of their own mental processes. Would it not, therefore, have better served the purpose of this study to have allotted less space to the Teutonic germ theory of the generation from 1876 to 1901, so as to have some space for the assumptions of the 1940's? Everyone who writes or studies history must confront the problem of human behavior and must accordingly make certain assumptions regarding psychology. An analysis of those commonly made— of the changes in them resulting from the development of the science of psychology in the recent past, and of their influence on the history being written—would be of more value to historical scholarship than the exceedingly good accounts of older assumptions no longer potent. In order to make such an analysis it would be necessary, among other things, not only to confront Freud but to understand him. In addition to the psychological assumptions, there are current many others that could be studied with profit. There is time to mention only one. It has persisted through the ages, yet it has not been adequately studied by writers on historiography. This is the assumption that the present is the culmination, the great summation to which the entire past has been moving. The egotism of the present controls the practice of many historians. The point is illustrated by the authors of this chapter when, referring to the present and their own generation of scholarship, they assert (p. 51), "With this practical recognition of the functional nature of historical knowledge, American historiography had come of age." Did not American history come of age when George Bancroft published his first volume in 1834, as Gooch said, using those very words, and will it not continue to "come of age" for every generation in the indefinite future?[3]

The third chapter, by Howard K. Beale, is a study of "What Historians Have Said about the Causes of the Civil War." This is the longest and probably the most instructive section of the book. No student or professor can fail to benefit from reading this judicious analysis of explanations, by various American historians, of the coming of the Civil War. At least it will make him temporarily humble in his own conclusions. At best it can make him aware of the complexity of causation in human affairs and of the need of historians for great wisdom as well as for erudition.

The fourth chapter, "Problems of Terminology in Historical Writing," consists of several pages of explanation by Charles A. Beard and more than twenty pages of definitions by Sidney Hook. The original plan was to collect from various histories numerous illustrations of the ways in which fifty words or terms were used, and then to have Hook correlate the results and formulate definitions as exact as possible. Unfortunately, it proved impossible to determine what was practice in the use of the selected words, and therefore only the definitions of Hook are presented. Without denying the value of epistemology and semantics as branches of knowledge and without minimizing the problems of terminology for historical

[3] G. P. Gooch, *History and Historians in the Nineteenth Century* (New York, 1913), p. 403.

scholarship, it can be doubted whether this section will materially aid historians in their teaching and writing. A definition of "Cause," occupying six printed pages, or one of "Understanding," spread over three pages, will probably not influence the practices of the historical profession. Indeed, the committee itself seems to have paid only slight attention to the section on terminology. Certainly, the definition given by the committee, in Proposition XIII, to the word "understanding" indicates little awareness of Hook's discussion. Beard seems to have been particularly concerned about the problems of terminology, although they are no different for a historian than for any other person who wishes to express thoughts in words and who has not a technical vocabulary. At one place (p. 136, n. 3) Beard and Vagts urge that the terms "cause" and "causality" should never be used in written history. It almost appears as if they thought that by eliminating the words they would eliminate the problem of causation.

The fifth and final chapter contains what is evidently the heart of the report of the Committee on Historiography. The committee, the chairman states, "assumed that every branch of knowledge presents or rests upon a number of propositions accepted by persons competent in such fields as valid in themselves and for application" (p. viii). Then, with rare courage, the committee proceeded to formulate the propositions in historiography which "could be accepted by the members of the committee as valid, as useful for the advancement of learning, and as worthy of submission to the judgment of historians in general." A draft of the propositions was sent to seventy historians for their comment. Only thirty-five of the seventy replied; of these, fifteen "did not seem to be opposed in any fundamental ways to the thought of the Propositions," twelve were willing to accept several of the propositions, and eight apparently rejected them altogether. After being revised in the light of the criticisms received, twenty-one propositions were agreed upon by the committee and were presented to the historical profession in its report.

Here is a challenge worthy of the serious thought of all of us who write or study or teach history. Eight scholars of high professional standing offer these twenty-one propositions as valid statements of the nature and limits of historiography. If they achieve the avowed purpose of the committee, there can be no excuse for a historian not knowing what he is doing. If these are in truth the propositions on which rests that branch of knowledge known as history, then we as students and writers of history need only to master them completely, and as teachers need only to see that our students also master them, in order to have more critical, more penetrating, and more fruitful history.

Would that this were so! Unfortunately, it is this part of the report, the most important part, the part where a unique and fundamental contribution was attempted, that is clearly a failure. The propositions reveal a lack of systematic thinking, a confusion in thought, a frequent internal inconsistency, and a vagueness, which make them useless. In their present form they probably perplex rather than clarify thought about history. The propositions include definitions, statements of fact, recommendations, and vague assertions of ideals and rules of method.[4] Some of the propositions overlap others; some seem to be irreconcilable with others; some are so platitudinous as to be meaningless.

These are extreme criticisms. To support them by an intensive analysis of the propositions individually and collectively would require a much longer time than that which is available. All that I can do is to illustrate with examples.

A vague assertion of an ideal so trite as to be valueless can be found in Proposition XV. It says, "The ideal which con-

[4] Definitions, XI, XIII; statements of fact, VIII; recommendations, IX, XVII; assertions of ideals, II, XV; rules of method V, XVI.

trols the historian in search of the utmost knowledge of the past is to achieve the most informed understanding of occurrences and personalities that available sources and discriminating imagination will permit, so as to write history with the highest possible degree of credibility." In the language of the undergraduate—"So, what?" All of us can subscribe to that ideal with no apparent danger and with no discernible benefit. Other propositions are equally bromidic. Proposition XX, for instance, says in effect that the historian must work in close and constant coöperation with specialists in the social sciences and the humanities, and even to some extent coördinate his work with that of the physical and biological sciences. How does such a statement advance the cause of scholarship, or clarify thought about history? One further illustration must suffice. The culmination of the discussion of generalizations and laws in Proposition XVI is the solemn admonition that "the important point in practice is to make historical work as exact as possible." When has any scholar suggested that historical work should not be as exact as possible!

What I meant when I said the propositions revealed confused rather than clear thinking can be illustrated by the first proposition. It says:

> The historian is one of the guardians of the cultural heritage of mankind. He is also an interpreter of the development of mankind. In carrying on these functions he aims to compose accurate accounts and analyses of selected portions of the past. From these accounts and analyses, or from the original sources themselves, he endeavors to reach generalizations that appear to be valid. On the basis of his knowledge he also seeks to provide credible explanations of the development of contemporary events, thoughts, manners, and institutions.

Just what this "basic premise" means, it is difficult to say. It could mean that if the historian does not seek "to provide credible explanations of the development of contemporary events, thought, manners, and institutions" he is no historian

and his work is not history. By this test many, if not most, of
the history books on our shelves are improperly classified.
If that last sentence means merely that the questions asked of
the historical sources will be those suggested by the present,
that meaning should be made clear. The previous sentence
should be clarified. If the sentence means that the historian
must endeavor to reach generalizations, there will be many to
challenge the proposition, and some would assert that the reverse is nearer the truth—that the historian in his endeavor to
establish particular events in the past employs generalizations
which he assumes to be true.

The lack of consistency between some of the propositions,
or at least the need of more explanation to reconcile them,
can be shown by comparing Proposition VI with Proposition
IX. Proposition VI states that every written history "is a
selection of facts made by some person or persons and is
ordered or organized under the influence of some scheme of
reference, interest, or emphasis—avowed or unavowed—in
the thought of the author or authors." Proposition IX, however, says, "Those who work in historiography in the scientific
spirit cannot embrace any of the absolutes put forth by
theologians or philosophers of any school as furnishing man-
dates by which the data of the past must be selected and organized or shaped to fit the institutional requirements of those
who espouse such absolutes." These two propositions present
a bothersome question. Of course, if Proposition IX means
merely that the historian must not blatantly select only the
facts which will conform to the philosophy of Karl Marx or of
St. Thomas Aquinas, most scholars would agree. But, if it
means precisely what it says, then there arises this difficulty—
what if that frame of reference, which Proposition VI asserts
every historian must have, is an absolute put forth by some
prevailing school of thought? What should Gibbon have
done? His frame of reference included the absolute of natural

law with all its implications, and yet the committee, in Proposition IX, wants him to divest himself of it. For that matter, has not the committee itself transgressed its own edict? Is not Proposition VI, with its assertion of the inevitability of some scheme of reference, an absolute of that philosophical school known as relativism?[5] Indeed, Proposition IX also is itself an absolute of a school of thought.

Enough has been said to indicate why I think the report of the committee fails in its major effort and why the propositions will not guide the profession of historians to a better understanding of what they are doing and hence to more satisfactory and more penetrating scholarship. But if the report is in this respect a failure, it is surely a glorious failure. No comparable challenge to the historians of America has been given unless it be the one that Henry Adams gave in his address as President of the American Historical Association in 1894. That challenge was ignored by our profession. We must not permit this one to share the same fate. Most certainly we agree with the committee that richer and more useful history would result if we were fully aware of our assumptions and of the nature and limits of historiography. As scholars responsible for the preservation and extension of a great branch of knowledge, we must start from where this committee stopped. In the report it is stated (p. 14) that "the Committee on Historiography, after long discussion, decided that neither the time nor the resources at its disposal would permit it to attempt a comprehensive treatment of the theme." In a matter so fundamental to historical scholarship the time and the resources necessary must be found. Both as individual scholars and especially as an organized profession we can contribute to this fundamental task. Careful, thorough planning will be required, as well as the best thought we can

---

[5] I am not objecting to this school of thought. Like so many in the present generation I frequently find myself subscribing to it.

muster from our ranks. The problem appears to be one which is peculiarly susceptible to the coöperative or team research which has been so fruitful in other branches of learning in recent years. The committee proceeded in this fashion, although they would, I am sure, be the first to agree that, in method as well as in conclusions, they made only tentative beginnings. It remains for the rest of us to carry on.

To suggest just one possibility, and in the hope of offering constructive criticism, I call attention to a serious problem confronting historical scholarship. It is not mentioned in the report, not even in the propositions concerned with method. This is the problem of coping with the plethora of materials in the modern period. Not many years ago the theory expounded to graduate students and unchallenged in the profession was that a scholar should examine all the source materials on his subject and should read all the secondary studies. By implication, at least, the Committee on Historiography endorsed this theory by stating in Proposition XV that the ideal "is to achieve the most informed understanding of occurrences and personalities that available sources . . . will permit."

Obviously, practice among historians of the modern period does not follow this theory, except when the historian confines himself strictly to a monograph on some small phase of a subject. Haphazard sampling and partial research which blandly omits large quantities of available source material are the rule rather than the exception today. This is the practice not of inferior scholars but of those whom we ourselves regard as our best. Not so many years ago, Henry F. Pringle's *Theodore Roosevelt* received high praise from the public and from the scholarly world. The praise was deserved, for the author, in addition to supplying a rich factual content, displayed a rare wisdom and a keen insight in his account of both the man and his times. Yet the briefest examination of his sources and bibliography will prove how far Pringle was from the scholarly theory that all available sources should be consulted. If there is any truth at all in the proposition that "he knows not England who only England knows," Pringle should have made researches in dozens of other manuscript collections available in the Library of Congress. I remember calling his attention to an item in the Senator Morgan papers and suggesting to him the desirability of going through that large collection. He replied that he had no time for it. He was right, of course; neither he nor any of us can know England if we set out first to know the rest of the world. Yet here is a problem to which historical scholars should find a clear and fruitful answer. And wouldn't even Pringle's excellent book have been better had he formulated a deliberate and informed policy of sampling or omission?

The same considerations apply to Arthur M. Schlesinger's *The Age of Jackson.* This history, too, is generally considered to be among the superior examples of recent scholarship. It has received the accolade of the Pulitzer prize, and deservedly so, if the reviews in scholarly journals are proper guides. Let me preface my adverse criticism by saying that I join the great majority in recognizing the merits of the book, although I would like to reverse the usual comment on George Bancroft —that in his history written in the 1880's he was still voting for Andrew Jackson—by pointing out that Schlesinger in his history of Andrew Jackson's period was voting for Franklin Roosevelt. The point is that again only a fraction of the source material available has been used. It is not that Schlesinger's research was inadequate. In fact, there have been few recent histories so firmly buttressed by extensive research. The bibliography extends over thirty printed pages and includes long lists of newspapers, pamphlets, magazines, and manuscript collections. Moreover, these items are used in the text. No scholar could be reasonably expected to assemble more data.

My question is directed to the method, or lack of method,

in selecting the materials used. In the bibliography, under the heading "The Jacksonian Tradition: Source Materials in Defense, Explanation and Reminiscence of Jacksonian Democracy," eighteen newspapers are listed. Except for one from Kentucky and one from Washington, D.C., the papers were all published in New England, New York, and Philadelphia. Under the heading "The Whig Tradition: Source Material in Opposition to Jackson," nineteen newspapers are listed. With the exception of three published in Washington, all are from Massachusetts and New York City. In the impressive list of manuscript collections used, the only ones not of men from New England, New York, and Philadelphia are those of Jackson, Taney, Polk, and Blair. Is it any wonder that the view is spreading that Jacksonian democracy was an eastern urban movement? Are these the proper sources for a history of *The Age of Jackson?* Even if the study were avowedly one of Jacksonian Democracy in Massachusetts, New York, and Philadelphia, why were these particular sources and not others chosen? Again, understanding would be promoted by an explicit declaration of method.

Perhaps the problem will be clarified by one more example. George E. Mowry's *Theodore Roosevelt and the Progressive Movement* is another study which has met the current standards of historical scholarship. Here again, there can be no complaint about the quantity of the research; it has obviously been extensive. One wonders, however, about the criteria which determined the selection of the data used, and about the methods followed in their use. For instance, except for the manuscript papers of Theodore Roosevelt (used extensively and intelligently), Knox, Bonaparte, and Carnegie, all the other collections are the papers of men who came from the states of the northern Mississippi Valley. Nearly all the manuscripts were located in that section—a fact which suggests that the sources used were chosen not solely for their significance to the history of Roosevelt and the Progressive movement but because of their accessibility to the University of Wisconsin, where Mowry submitted a draft of his book as a dissertation. A dozen other collections of manuscripts at the Library of Congress and elsewhere could be readily named, which are fully as significant for the subject as any of the collections used except the Roosevelt papers. No statement of method is given to explain why such sources were ignored or why the ones used were selected. Similarly, no explanation of method is made to justify the use made of newspapers. Here is Mowry's practice. In chapter iii, entitled, "The Cause Célèbre: Pinchot-Ballinger," the following papers are cited: Des Moines *Register and Leader,* seven times; Kansas City *Star,* six times; *La Follette's Weekly,* twice; Philadelphia *North American,* twice; and the New York *Times,* Milwaukee *Sentinel,* and the Chicago *Tribune,* once each. In chapter vi, entitled "Progressive Politics," the papers used are: the New York *Times,* eight times; the New York *Sun,* seven times; the Des Moines *Register and Leader* and the Kansas City *Star,* six times each; *La Follette's Weekly,* three times; the Philadelphia *North American,* twice; and the Chicago *Tribune* and the Chicago *Inter Ocean,* one each. In chapter ix, entitled "We Stand at Armageddon," the papers cited are: the New York *Times,* fifteen citations; the New York *Sun,* eleven; Kansas City *Star,* seven; New York *World,* four; Philadelphia *North American,* three; *La Follette's Weekly,* one. In chapter xii, entitled "Wilson and War," the only paper cited is the New York *Times,* which is used ten times.[6] Why there should be this remarkable shift in the newspapers used as sources is left completely to the reader's conjecture. Why the papers of the Middle West were selected as sources for the account of the Pinchot-Ballinger episode, and why the New York papers

---

[6] My own method of sampling was to select chapters iii, vi, ix, and xii without previous examination.

were used for the discussion of the great crisis in the Republican National Convention is not stated, if indeed there was any deliberate plan at all.

Let me repeat, these three histories are among the most highly regarded by the present generation of scholars. It is the standards of the profession which need formulation and clarification so that both the writer and the reader will know precisely what is being done and why. A historian confronted by more source material than can be read within a lifetime, or within reasonable limits, must resort to sampling. Scholarly standards should require him to adopt deliberately some method of sampling and to state explicitly what it is and how it operates. A committee which will formulate a new theory to supplant the outmoded theory of all source material and all secondary studies would render a great service to historical scholarship. Before making such an attempt a very comprehensive analysis of present practice should be made. There should also be a full knowledge of the experience of physicists and mathematicians with sampling as a means of establishing truth.

If work of this type is not undertaken, if the profession does not grapple with the basic problems raised but by no means settled by the Committee on Historiography, we shall have failed to meet one of our most obvious responsibilities.

The Education of Historians in the United States

ON NUMEROUS OCCASIONS the Carnegie Foundation or Corporation has supported studies of the training required for admission to various professions. The most notable of these important contributions was Abraham Flexner's report in 1910 on medical education, which had a profound impact on that profession. Consequently, it was natural to turn to the Carnegie Corporation when the American Historical Association, the major organization of the historical profession in the United States, decided that a study of the recruitment and training of new members of the profession was urgently needed. The requested funds were provided, and a committee of six prominent scholars, with Dexter Perkins as chairman, assumed responsibility for the project. Professor John Snell, on leave from Tulane University for two years, acted as director of the study, visiting many graduate schools, where he interviewed both faculty and students, and doing the research that made possible this first intensive and careful report on *The Education of Historians in the United States.*[1] Of the ten

[1] Dexter Perkins, John L. Snell, and the Committee on Graduate Education of the American Historical Association, *The Education of Historians in the United States* (New York, 1962).

chapters, Snell wrote all but the introduction, which was written by Perkins, and the last, which contains the recommendations of the committee.

Now facts supported by many statistical tables are available to guide thought and action. Now students and faculty can compare their situation and practices not necessarily with what are the wisest possible solutions but with those that are currently prevailing in the profession. Naturally, the statistics must be used with the grains of salt scholars customarily apply, with the knowledge that they, however accurate, may be inadequate bases on which to erect large generalizations. In some cases they are themselves necessarily merely estimates. This is notably the case in Chapter II, in which Snell forecasts the number of college teachers of history that will be needed in the near future. He makes a convincing case for his conclusion that the number, while large, will not be as great as has frequently been predicted and will not compel emergency measures.

Next comes a chapter devoted to graduate students in history. Do they compare favorably in quality with those in other fields? The answer is "no" except when compared with "other social science majors." What do they report as the most serious inadequacies in their undergraduate preparation? The leading item is foreign language training. Where do they come from? They typically received their baccalaureate degrees from large institutions. "All but four of the 25 largest undergraduate producers of history Ph.D.s between 1936 and 1956 were large institutions." If the sample of 182 recipients of the Ph.D. in 1958 is an accurate index, one was a Negro, two were Orientals, 10 per cent were women; 63 per cent came from Protestant families, 20 per cent from Catholic, and 13 per cent from Jewish; two-thirds were married males, and 44 per cent had children; 1 per cent were under twenty-six years of age, 75 per cent had passed their thirtieth birthday, and 35 per cent their thirty-sixth. Their parents were not products of higher education; only 31 per cent of the fathers and 18 per cent of the mothers had received bachelor's degrees, and 40 per cent of the fathers and 37 per cent of the mothers had not completed high school. Perhaps those facts explain the further fact that only 24 per cent of the graduate students in 1958 were receiving financial aid from their parents. Aid was relatively scanty from other sources. Both in number and in size, the stipends received by graduate students in history were smaller than those received by students in the other social sciences and of course than those by students in the sciences. More than half the Ph.D.'s of 1958 had worked full time for more than one academic year between beginning graduate study and the award of the degree.

Following two chapters, one devoted to the teaching of history in the colleges and one to the master's degree, are four on the Ph.D. degree, which constitute the heart of the report. The first of these contains much significant data. There were, in 1960, apparently eighty-eight institutions that had programs leading to the Ph.D. degree in history. Seven universities, probably assisted by the National Defense Education Act, initiated programs after 1958. Two other institutions awarded no degrees in the eleven years, 1948-1958. Others were not active, four granting only one degree each in the eleven-year period. In fact, twenty-seven of the seventy-nine universities granting degrees averaged fewer than one degree a year. Harvard, including Radcliffe, produced 377 of 3,133 degrees in the period, or more than the combined production of the forty-two smallest producers. Columbia, with 288 degrees, produced more than the thirty-eight smallest producers. The eighteen largest producers awarded 67 per cent of all the Ph.D.'s of the period, and the twenty-eight largest producers awarded 81 per cent of the total.

Some interesting facts emerge from the analysis of the Ph.D.

degrees granted by fields and by geographical sections of the country. Of the 1,458 degrees awarded in the five years, 1955-1959, just over half (748 or 51 per cent) were in United States history. The twenty-nine institutions in the East granted 45 per cent of their degrees in United States history; the seventeen institutions in the South granted 69 per cent; for the seventeen institutions in the Midwest the figure was 52 per cent; and for the eleven institutions in the West, 51 per cent. The southern universities also concentrated on Latin American history since 31 of the 68 degrees granted were from southern institutions. In fact, one southern university, Texas, gave 15 degrees in Latin American history or more than all of the universities of the West (11), or the Midwest (10), and almost equal to all from the East (16). The southern universities granted no degree in ancient history, the western only 1, the midwestern and eastern 5 each, making a total of 11 or about 2 a year for the entire country. Obviously that field of knowledge is in danger of drying up.

In the same chapter are statistics showing the teaching loads in the graduate institutions, the size of classes, and the library resources. The last, it is pointed out, are lamentably low in the seven universities that have inaugurated Ph.D. programs since 1958, even much lower than in the thirty-six universities rated in third rank as centers of Ph.D. training in history.

There is a chapter on the kinds of programs in use: the nature and number of fields required, the lecture and seminar courses offered, the part played by the doctoral dissertation (should it be a publishable book?), and the examinations generally required.

All of us in the profession and especially those in graduate institutions can find much in the chapter on the major criticisms of training for the Ph.D. degree. Both graduate students and employers of the new Ph.D.'s complain that not enough teaching has been included in the graduate program. A second widespread criticism is aimed at overspecialization and its converse, the absence of breadth. The third major criticism is on the length of time it takes to attain a Ph.D. degree. All of these points are hackneyed, but precise data are made available so that a more enlightened discussion is possible.

More valuable because the contents are less well known is the unfortunately short chapter on experiments being made at various universities. Although no radically different or fundamentally new features are incorporated, efforts are being made by a number of graduate departments to alleviate the most obvious existing difficulties. Some of these attempts to include experience in teaching, to make courses and examinations more meaningful, and to shorten the time involved are described. It is hoped that they will be noted and adopted.

The committee's recommendations in the final chapter will not, I believe, have an impact on the profession comparable to that which Flexner's report had on the medical profession. The opportunity for reform is not as great because the historical profession and the educational system by which its new members are trained are not in the deplorable condition of medical education before Flexner. As long as so large a percentage of the profession receive their training in universities that by common consent are among the best, the situation is relatively good. Yet, there is pressing need for improvement, and the recommendations of the committee must be judged in this context. Everyone will readily accept in principle the standards set by the committee. In many cases, they are like sermons against sin and are as ineffective. Who could object to the recommendation that "Ph.D. candidates should write dissertations on significant subjects, even though they may explore in detail only one aspect or a few aspects of a large topic"? But will present practice be affected?

In discussing the need to reduce the period of graduate study the committee, after stating its belief that the degree "should require no more than four academic years for most full-time Ph.D. candidates, including study for the master's degree and the completion of the Ph.D. dissertation" and after noting that the major cause of delay "is most often the financial inability of students to undertake full-time study," recommends that more nonduty fellowships and scholarships be made available. The committee further notes that many students are delayed by difficulty in passing foreign language examinations. Their solution is to suggest that the knowledge be acquired during undergraduate years and that an examination in one language be required before admittance to graduate school or by the beginning of the second year of graduate study, and in the second language by the beginning of the second year and in any case by the beginning of the third year. On the subject of length of the thesis, which has also become a serious cause of delay, the committee recommends that it should be restricted sufficiently to permit the student to do the research and writing in one calendar year of full-time work and that it "usually need not be longer than 300 typed pages." Snell stated that history theses in 1957-1958 averaged 351 pages. Will all this exhortation result in any reduction in the length of graduate study for future members of the profession? I doubt it.

On one very important subject the committee differs from Snell's recommendations. The committee asserts that three conditions "should be met by history departments that offer Ph.D. training." These are: the department should have faculty members in at least three broad fields of history, the majority of whom must be experienced teachers whose "scholarly research contributions are recognized by fellow historians in the nation"; "financial resources for the assistance of graduate students, allocation of faculty time, and the development of faculty members as scholars"; and library resources "adequate for training in research seminars and for preparation for the general examination." Snell is both more specific and more exacting. He maintains that a department should have at least ten members in at least five broad fields of history, most of whom are recognized by fellow specialists, and adequate funds and library resources which, he urges, should exceed those of most of the seven newest universities offering the doctorate.

This leads me to a final comment. Suppose, under the pressure of a real or anticipated acute shortage of Ph.D.'s in history, many of the present weak or new and still weaker institutions begin granting degrees in large numbers. How can the standards of the profession be protected? The committee does not discuss that possibility. It is probably assumed that the competition of the market place will be adequate protection. I wonder if it is.

Part II

United States Foreign Relations:

An Historian's Concern

The United States

and the Defense of the Western Hemisphere,

1815-1940

ONE OF THE essential facts, if indeed it was not the most basic fact, in the situation that produced the original Monroe Doctrine was the existence of a distinct European system. The great continental powers of Europe united in suppressing with force the appearance of any of the ideas of the French Revolution in any of the countries of Europe. If extended to the new world this system of intervention in the internal affairs of other countries and of dictating the political institutions other peoples might employ would have seriously endangered the United States. An application of the system to Latin America would have left the United States the last bulwark of those ideas in the world, a more or less democratic republic, born of the successful assertion of a right of revolution, and with a government based on the precise political philosophy which was anathema to the European powers.

Of course the system was not extended to the Western Hemisphere. In fact it broke down in Europe itself within a comparatively short time. In 1830 it failed to function, and by 1848 it had clearly disintegrated beyond hope of restoration. From then until the 1930's there was no European system of the character Monroe referred to in his message. In this respect the political system of Europe was essentially the same as that of America. Consequently the Monroe Doctrine lost the most valid of its original reasons for existence. Other reasons there might be, but they rested on different grounds. For example, the American antipathy to the French intervention in Mexico in the 1860's arose, so far as it was not blind devotion to a traditional policy, not from the belief that there was any European system which, if extended to America, would endanger the United States but from the fear of having a powerful and aggressive neighbor. It was therefore not as close to the original Monroe Doctrine as to what might be called the Jefferson Doctrine—the policy of resisting the appearance in Louisiana in 1802 of a powerful and aggressive power. Although no writer has adequately traced the significance of the disappearance of a European system for the ideological background of the Monroe Doctrine, an appreciation of the fact was one of the reasons why there has been an increasing criticism among scholars of the Doctrine as an outmoded policy the reasons for which have ceased to exist.

Be that as it may, it is clear that today there is again a European system in the sense that the dominant powers on the continent are interfering in the internal affairs of other countries to crush with force political institutions based on a hostile philosophy. When Mussolini announced that Italy could not tolerate the existence of the republican government in Spain, he was speaking a language that would have been understood by the leaders of the Holy Alliance. Again England alone of the great European powers is opposing the system. Again it is widely believed in the United States that the extension of the system of the new and unholy alliance to the Western Hemisphere would endanger the peace and safety of the United States. The raison d'etre of the original Monroe Doctrine has been restored.

There is this contrast between the two periods: in Monroe's time it was the counter-revolution which threatened the United States. The revolution itself proclaimed a political philosophy which had already been adopted in the United States, where even the conservatives on the extreme right however much they might detest popular sovereignty in practice were committed to it and kindred principles in theory. In the present period it is the revolution which challenges the American political philosophy. It is a revolutionary movement even though it is obviously entangled with the lust for power of Hitler and his group, who claim to be the defenders or bitter opponents of capitalism with equal facility. It is a revolutionary challenge to existing institutions and philosophy precisely as the French Revolution was even after it became entangled with Napoleon's lust for power.

Given a distinct European system which might possibly be extended by force to the Western Hemisphere, and which would, if so extended, endanger the peace and safety of the peoples of the New World, proposals for an American system which provide for united action in defense were and are to be expected. They did in fact appear. There have been three major occasions when the American government and people have been confronted with the question of whether or not they would coöperate with the other American governments in defending the Western Hemisphere.

The first time the policy was presented for decision was in the period ending with the abortive Panama Congress of 1826. It is unnecessary to review the unfortunate history of that Congress both because it is well known and because most of it is irrelevant to the present discussion. Whether or not Bolivar wished to erect a hemispheric system including the United States, or a Hispanic American confederation excluding the United States, or a liberal system embracing England as well as the New World; whether or not British influence favored the proposal; whether or not British rivalry with the United States for leadership in Latin American politics was the dominant factor—all these are alike irrelevant. The facts that are both clear and germane are these. The initiative came from Latin America. England was invited not because of Canada but because of the British opposition to European intervention in the New World. The purpose, or at least one of the major purposes, of the proposed Congress was considered by many in Latin America and by even more in the United States to be the establishment of some sort of hemispheric organization for defense. The various treaties of alliance between Latin American countries could be renewed and extended, while the United States might enter the organization by transforming the general policy of Monroe's message into specific commitments for action.[1]

To this proposal the United States, as is well known, answered in unmistakable terms. There were a few individual citizens of the United States who at one time or another had favored joint action with Latin America for the defense of the two continents. Indeed, the very man who was Secretary of State in 1826 had warmly advocated an American defensive system in 1817. But since then, either events or the responsibility of office had caused him to abandon such a program. He had joined with President Adams in rejecting the offers of individual Latin American countries to enter into alliances for resisting European aggression, as contemplated by the Monroe Doctrine. The administration, as Adams made perfectly clear when requesting Congress to sanction the participation of the United States in the Panama Congress, rejected with equal or even greater firmness any suggestion of a hemispheric alli-

[1] The most extensive account of these events is J. B. Lockey, *Pan-Americanism: Its Beginnings* (New York, 1920). It should be supplemented by J. Fred Rippy, *Rivalry of the United States and Great Britain over Latin America* (Baltimore, 1929), pp. 217-246.

ance or organization for purposes of defense. The Monroe Doctrine was to be a strictly unilateral affair. The same views dominated the Congress of the United States. In fact in the long debates in both the Senate and the House not only was the idea of joint defense repudiated but there were expressions of positive aversion to entering with Latin American countries into any commitments regarding the Monroe Doctrine.[2]

Nearly a century was to elapse before the government and people of the United States faced the issue again.[3] In that long interim a number of significant changes took place. The United States became one of the great powers of the world. Canada became a dominion of the British Commonwealth of Nations. The European system, which had threatened the peace and safety of the peoples in this hemisphere, completely disappeared. Nevertheless the Monroe Doctrine remained. Indeed it loomed larger than ever both in the eyes of the United States and in those of Latin America. No longer confronted with a hostile European system, Latin America feared aggression from the United States more than from any individual country of Europe. Under such circumstances proposals for hemispheric organization for defense were not likely to come from Latin America. Nor did any come from the United States. The government of the United States did, in the latter half of the century, supply the initiative for a Pan-American movement, but that movement had nothing to do with the defense of the hemisphere. Its objects were the promotion of peace between the countries of the hemisphere and the

[2] The best treatment of this phase is Dexter Perkins, *The Monroe Doctrine, 1823-1826* (Cambridge, 1927).

[3] This statement is subject to qualification. Suggestions for joint action in defense of the hemisphere were advanced by individuals from time to time. During the French intervention in Mexico in the 1860's several Latin American countries initiated proposals for the cooperative defense of the Monroe Doctrine, but Seward rejected all such advances so firmly and so quickly that the issue did not reach the public. Dexter Perkins, *The Monroe Doctrine, 1826-1867* (Baltimore, 1933), pp. 459-461.

promotion of closer cultural and scientific relations. However laudable the Pan-American movement might be, it clearly did not represent a change in the policy of the United States for resisting attacks on America from the outside world. That policy remained just as it had been in 1826.

A complete reversal in policy was to be proposed soon after the outbreak of the World War in 1914 shocked people in the United States from their complacent ignorance of international politics and made them, or some of them, willing to adopt radically different policies to meet what they now saw were the realities of the situation. The first news of a proposed new policy for hemispheric defense reached the public through a speech President Wilson delivered to a Pan-American Scientific Congress meeting in Washington on January 6, 1916. After developing the idea that there existed a community of political interest in the Western Hemisphere, Wilson suggested that the States of America should unite in guaranteeing absolutely to each other political independence and territorial integrity. The contemplated revolution in policy thus publicly announced had been initiated by Wilson more than a year earlier. According to the account based on the journal and letters of Colonel House it was House who originated the plan and persuaded Wilson of its wisdom.[4] Others, however, had reached the same conclusion before House. Thus Andrew Carnegie urged Wilson to banish war from the American continent by taking the lead in forming a league of the twenty-one republics. The fragment of his letter which has been published does not indicate whether the league was to banish war by coöperating in the defense of the hemisphere or merely by refraining from wars against each other.[5] Still

[4] Charles Seymour, *The Intimate Papers of Colonel House* (Boston, 1926), I, 207-210.
[5] Ray Stannard Baker, *Woodrow Wilson, Life and Letters* (Garden City, N.Y., 1927), VI, 83.

earlier a member of the House of Representatives, James L. Slayden of Texas, had proposed a mutual guarantee by the nations of this hemisphere of territorial integrity and of sovereignty, and Wilson's attention was drawn to his suggestion.[6] In fact, strange as it may seem, former President Theodore Roosevelt had made some recommendations to the same effect. In a speech at Rio de Janeiro in 1913 he declared that the nations of Latin America "sufficiently advanced" "should participate on an absolute equality in the responsibilities and development" of the Monroe Doctrine and that "it must be made a continental and not a unilateral doctrine."

Whatever the source of the policy, Wilson adopted it in December of 1914 for various reasons, some of which were not directly concerned with the defense of the hemisphere. There is no doubt that the new policy was in part designed to remove Latin American fears of the United States. As is shown by the provisions of the Pan-American Pact, of which it was the principal clause, it was also intended to promote peace between the countries in the Western Hemisphere. It had still another objective. Both Colonel House and Wilson recorded their belief that by welding the two continents of the Americas together into such a system they could "show the way to the rest of the world as to how to make a basis of peace."[7]

These hopes were not to be realized. Colonel House, armed with a copy of the essential points typed, as usual, by Wilson himself, sought the ambassadors of Argentina, Brazil, and Chile, for it had been thought best to secure the approval of the A B C powers before submitting the projected treaty to the smaller republics. The Argentine ambassador, Colonel House reported, was "tremendously impressed with the signi-

[6] Harley Notter, *The Origins of the Foreign Policy of Woodrow Wilson* (Baltimore, 1937), pp. 273-274. See also Baker, *op. cit.*, IV, 285.
[7] Notter, *op. cit.*, 374; Seymour, *op. cit.*, I, 209.

ficance of the [mutual guarantee]," saying "it struck a new note and would create an epoch in governmental affairs." When told the President himself had typed the memorandum, "he asked permission to keep it, saying it would become an historical document of much value."[8]

It might in truth have become such, if the other Latin American countries had replied as favorably and as promptly as the Argentine Republic. Brazil did so, but the Chilean government, perhaps because of its pending boundary dispute with Peru, made only an ambiguous reply, favoring in principle but objecting in fact. Nevertheless the project was pushed by Wilson, House, and Lansing, and there were periods when success seemed just around the corner. Colonel House without apparently consulting either the Latin American countries or his own President suggested to Sir Edward Grey that the British Government might join the American system of mutual guarantees, as far as their American colonies were concerned. With a more cautious sense of responsibility Grey consulted the Canadian government and found it willing to have him say what he had wished to say in favor of the Pan-American pact.

The high tide of this attempt to organize the Western Hemisphere for defense had been reached. Continued evasion by Chile, the unfavorable atmosphere created by the Pershing expedition into Mexico, the presidential election in the United States, and finally the entry of the United States into the war all contributed to the abandonment of the plan.

The American public had evinced surprisingly little interest in the whole affair considering the fact that one of its oldest and most important foreign policies was to be reversed. One would have expected that there would have been fiery debates in the Senate during the weeks immediately following Wilson's speech of January 6, 1916, when he first publicly announced

[8] *Ibid.*, p. 213.

his proposal for mutual guarantees. There were no debates at all on the subject. Senator Borah spoke at some length, but instead of denouncing entangling alliances he urged intervention in Mexico. Indeed the only reference in any way connected with the problem of Latin American relations, except those relating to Mexico, was a resolution introduced in the Senate the day after Wilson's speech stating that the Senate "would view with pleasure negotiations on the part of the President with Central and South American countries to agree upon a day to be celebrated . . . as Pan American Day." A little over three weeks after Wilson's speech the *Literary Digest* ran an article quoting newspaper comment on the speech. The *Digest* reported that some papers favored his plan and some papers opposed it. What it surprising is that most of the comment quoted was not on the important issue but on the minor question of whether or not the United States should agree to prohibit the exportation of munitions of war to revolutionists.

Neither public apathy nor Chilean opposition caused Wilson to abandon his plan. In fact it is incorrect to say that Wilson abandoned the policy of organizing the hemisphere for defense. On the contrary he merged it into the larger scheme of organizing the world for the defense of all governments everywhere. The Pan-American guarantee became Article 10 of the Covenant of the League of Nations. Wilson ceased working for an American system because it would be unnecessary in the world system he was constructing. There had been no indication in the preliminary negotiations for the Pan-American Pact that Wilson and the others contemplated any hemispheric governmental machinery such as the later League of Nations for the world. Inevitably some such machinery would have resulted. As Article 10 was the heart of the League, the mutual guarantee would have been the heart of an American system of defense. A heart cannot function

without a body. Hemispheric political instruments and organization were implicit in the project.

When the small minority of irreconcilables in the Senate,
aided by political factors and by a confused and leaderless
public opinion, drove the large majority in the Senate to reject
the Versailles Treaty, they blocked any participation by the
United States in that world organization for defense. With
the greater went the lesser. There was to be no organization of
the Western Hemisphere for its defense. At the moment with
all Europe exhausted by the efforts of the World War there
was no imminent danger, and in any case, public opinion in
the United States had reversed its recent direction. It and the
United States government returned to the policy of 1826.
The Monroe Doctrine was to be strictly unilateral. No commitments, no agreements for coöperative action were to be
made with Latin American countries.

Not everyone in the United States accepted this decision as
final, and for the first time in our history a significant but
largely inchoate mass of opinion wanted the opposite policy.
Usually they thought in terms not solely of hemispheric coöperation for defense but of world-wide organization and action to defend peace. Their views produced no practical results. Neither did any responsible official in any part of the
United States government, at least so far as available records
indicate, give any consideration to the several proposals for
hemispheric defensive organization which originated in Latin
America during the period immediately after the war. The
government of the United States did in the postwar period and
especially in the postdepression years make strenuous efforts
to eliminate Latin American fears and suspicions of the United States. But these, which have been partially successful,
had no connection with the defense of the two continents.

Events drifted until it became increasingly apparent: first,
that the League organization for collective security had failed,

and second, that a new system was being riveted on Europe by force, a system which, like the one of 1815-26, meant war and intervention in the internal affairs of other countries. The objects were not only economic loot but were also the destruction of political institutions disliked by the proponents of the new system. This was because the totalitarian philosophy represented a revolutionary movement and was fanatically and sincerely professed by some. It challenged the philosophy of the Western Hemisphere as well as that of western Europe. There was wealth, too, in the new world.

The war because of its character and because of the proportions it assumed again raised the issue of organizing the Western Hemisphere for defense and drove the United States and Latin America to some joint action. It is clear that so far Pan-American coöperation has been divided into two distinct periods. The first ended in June, 1940. During it the public and the government of the United States and, almost certainly, Latin America as well, agreed with the French General Staff that this was the war of 1914 over again. There were no serious doubts of the ultimate victory of the Allies and no serious fears for the safety of the two American continents. During this period there was relatively little joint action, for hemispheric organization has varied directly with Hitler's fortunes in Europe, and the dominant desire was to preserve neutrality and avoid incidents. Thus even before the war assumed the form of fighting between armies it had been agreed at the Lima Pan-American Congress in 1938 that the republics of the hemisphere would consult together if their security appeared to be in danger. In September, 1939, the foreign ministers of the New World met at Panama and drew up a Declaration of Neutrality which attempted to set forth the standards of conduct they proposed to follow as neutral states and the Declaration of Panama which attempted, though not very successfully, to create a safety belt of three hundred miles around the Western Hemisphere. At Panama they also established an Inter-American Neutrality Committee and an Inter-American Financial and Economic Advisory Committee. Yet in this first period the tendency was to seek parallel action by individual countries rather than joint action, and there was little need to take positive and drastic action. It is true that just at the end of the period when Uruguay had fifth column difficulties Brazil supplied rifles and the United States sent two cruisers there on a visit. These were demonstrations of solidarity but were not done in the name or specifically by the authority of any hemispheric body.[9]

An entirely new atmosphere dominated the second and hurriedly called meeting of the foreign ministers which met at Havana in July of 1940. France had collapsed, Hitler was the conqueror of the continent, and the defeat of Great Britain within a brief period was widely expected. The New World had to adjust itself to a new international situation. The British navy was in danger for the first time since there had been an independent America. For the first time the significance of the British control of the Atlantic was appreciated and the impact of the shocking idea that it might soon end shattered many traditional and complacent policies. Hemispheric organization for defense became a more vital matter and more of a reality. Perhaps the most significant single fact was the decision that "If a non-American State shall directly or indirectly attempt to replace another non-American State in the sovereignty or control which it exercised over any territory located in America, thus threatening the peace of the continent such territory" should be put under a provisional regime in the name of all the Pan-American countries and under an Inter-American Commission on Territorial Admin-

[9] For the account of these recent events the sources used are news releases of the Department of State, the newspapers, and the valuable pamphlets published by the Foreign Policy Association.

istration. In other words, the mandate concept of the League of Nations was applied, and there was provision for real hemispheric control. The Monroe Doctrine, certainly one important part of it, had been continentalized. The new attitude prevailing at Havana was reflected in decisions to consult on fifth column dangers and above all in a declaration that aggression against one American republic was to be considered aggression against all. To implement this principle it was recommended that the American republics should enter into further agreements to insure coöperation in defense. Not much has yet been done in this field, but steps comparable to the arrangement between the United States and Canada are obviously intended. The plan is truly hemispheric, Canada being linked through its joint action with the United States, and the British colonies through the naval-base–destroyer deal.

From the beginning of the war the initiative has been supplied by the United States. The policy of 1826 has been abandoned without protest from Congress or public. The Monroe Doctrine is no longer strictly unilateral, and the United States is anxious to enter into agreements to organize the entire hemisphere for defense. Whether or not this return to Wilson's policy is permanent, whether or not the improvised commissions and other bodies will develop into the political machinery of an American League of Nations, how much further the present tendencies will go will all depend on the course of events in Europe. The organization of the Western Hemisphere for defense, like so much else that is of value in our lives, depends upon the British ability to withstand the attacks of Hitler.

Uncle Sam as Deer, Jackal, and Lion

OR

The United States in Power Politics

THERE IS a persistent, widespread, and dangerous belief in the United States that power politics is a wicked European institution from which we have remained aloof during most of our history. With this comforting assumption of moral superiority there is always the determination that we must continue to stay out of power politics—if for no other reason, because power politics breeds war. Woodrow Wilson expressed the traditional American view when in a speech in 1917 he referred to "the great game, now forever discredited," yet, as will appear, Wilson himself instinctively and deliberately played the game when he felt national interests would thereby be promoted. Henry Wallace included power politics among the other things to which he objected in his notorious Madison Square address. In so doing he was certain to receive the approval of his audience, for practically any American audience, at least during the past seventy-five years, would have applauded a denunciation of power politics. The American people have repeatedly joined in thanking God that we, because of our geographical isolation and because of our resistance to the temptation of conquest, have escaped this curse of humanity which has flourished with such disastrous consequences in Europe and the rest of the world.

So axiomatic is this belief in America it has rarely been subjected to any analysis. Yet tested either by general considerations or by the facts of world history or, curiously enough, by the facts of American history itself, the belief is untenable.

The theoretical objections to the prevailing American view of power politics can be stated briefly. The choice is not power or no power. There can be no organized society without power being present and active. Power can be, has been, compared to gravitation. Many people have fallen out of windows or down mountains suffering painful injuries or death, yet without gravity there would be no world or life. Power can accurately be regarded as both essential and beneficial. All law, all civilization, all freedom depend on the existence of power. The question, Mr. Churchill has correctly stated, is not power or no power, but who is to have the power and for what purpose is it to be used.

Power politics would not have its bad reputation if it were called "the politics of not being overpowered," as Schwarzschild proposed in his *Primer of the Coming World*. That name is equally justified. If power politics means conquest by some it also means national independence and freedom for others. These desirable results are attained by the balance-of-power system which is the method by which the game of politics to prevent being overpowered is played. Whenever any nation or group of nations becomes so powerful it can and does dictate to other and less powerful nations, the latter will eventually try to combine to establish an agglomeration of power sufficient to resist the threat. The balance-of-power system has preserved the independence of nations of the world. The small nations live by it. The people of Holland, of Turkey, and of many other nations undoubtedly regard the balance of power system of power politics as their sole bulwark against extinction and not as something evil and sinful.

Why nations should wish so desperately to preserve their national independence is not easy to explain. It is one of the inevitable characteristics of nationalism, and like other aspects of nationalism defies rational explanation. Nationalism is a sentiment, a belief, a consciousness of belonging to one group distinct from and often hostile to all other national groups. Man belongs to many groups—economic such as labor unions or manufacturers' associations, religious, social, scientific, and professional. Yet the national group is the one to which he gives ultimate allegiance. When the test comes it prevails, proletarian shoots proletarian, capitalist shoots capitalist, Catholic kills Catholic, and scientist his fellow scientist. A man from Mars, or a detached philosopher, could easily regard such human behavior as illogical. The highly educated and economically favored professional man in Germany had much more in common with the highly educated and economically favored professional man in France, England, or the United States than any of them had with the peasant or tenant farmer or industrial laborer in his own country. These professional men talk the same mental language (medicine, physics, or music), they read the same literature, know the same music, look at the same art, dress in the same kind of clothes, live in the same kind of houses and by the same mores, yet they give their ultimate allegiance to the national group. It is the peasants and workers with whom they feel identity rather than with the other professional men. Similarly the workers of the world have refused to unite and instead have acted along national lines.

What causes nationalism—this consciousness of belonging to an all-important group which triumphs over every other loyalty—I do not know, nor have I ever seen an adequate explanation. Certainly a common language is not a decisive factor; witness Canada or Switzerland each with one nation but several languages, or the United States and England with one language and two nations. Nor is geography decisive, as Ireland and the Iberian peninsula demonstrate—for two nations exist where geography says one should—or Poland proves with no natural geographic boundaries. Economic interests are not decisive nor is a common history. Indeed nationalistic historians will invent a history in any case. But if its origin is in doubt, there can be no doubt as to this one great result of nationalism. Each group is determined at all costs to have its own national government, however bad, and finds rule by the people of another nation an intolerable tyranny. In behalf of national independence life and property will be sacrificed, and have been by French and Germans, and Russians and Americans, as well as by Belgians and Dutch and Norwegians.

The nationalist who feels his nation in danger inevitably and hopefully turns to the balance-of-power system or power politics. For him it is a beneficent institution.

Whether sinful or beneficent, the American people from the beginning of our history to the present have been participants in the game of power politics, and the course of our history has depended on it. Our status in power politics has changed in the course of time. First we were the stakes of diplomacy, one of the prizes over which big powers fought, the deer hunted by the powerful beasts of prey. Then we became for a century or more the jackal who lives and prospers on the power politics of the truly great, who picks up what he can but does not play a dominant role. Finally we attained the stature of a lion, a ruler of that jungle which is international power politics.

About the career of the American people as deer little need be said. The colonies became one of the rich stakes of diplomacy. Mercantilist theory made most of the statesmen of Europe think of colonial wealth and colonial trade as the true source of national power. Consequently wars were begun to extend or capture colonies in the New World and the victor was apt to estimate his winnings by the new map of America which resulted. The European wars, all of which were part of power politics and the balance-of-power system, were re-enacted in America. The colonists of each government went to war when their governments in Europe went to war. Being members of the nation, this involvement in power politics seemed as natural to them as the rise and fall of the tides or the movement of the heavenly bodies. It would have required the emergence of a new nationalism or at least the disappearance of English nationalism to have caused the colonists to question the wisdom of their participation in English wars. There is no evidence that any aversion to the consequences of power politics played any part in the movement for independence. This is true in spite of the fact that Tom Paine, a recent immigrant from England who was an eighteenth-century internationalist, urged that point in *Common Sense,* where he wrote "any submission to, or dependence on, Great Britain tends directly to involve this continent in European wars and quarrels; and set us at variance with nations, who would otherwise seek our friendship, and against whom we have neither anger nor complaint."

It was for other reasons, not aversion to power politics, that the Americans declared their independence, and in so doing changed from deer to jackal. The career of the United States as jackal was highly successful. One great prize after another was won with little effort and at little risk. While the huge lions fought costly battles or watched each other with snarling suspicion, the clever jackal making the most of each situation snatched what he wanted and grew mightily.

No antipathy to power politics restrained the Americans

who declared their independence in 1776. Without hesitation they plunged into the very center of the game of power politics, assumed its risks, and came out the only winner. Theirs may well have been the courage of desperation. Only power politics and the balance-of-power system could make it possible to withstand the strength of Great Britain, then the dominant power in the world. The paradox is that if Great Britain had not been so powerful the Americans would not have received any help from France and Europe. There had to be some compelling reason to induce absolutist France to help revolutionists who proclaimed the doctrine that governments derive their powers from the consent of the governed and that the people have a right to abolish a government which is tyrannical. Such ideas were incompatible with the existence of that French government and those very ideas were soon to end that French government and the life of that king. Fortunately for the Americans the exigencies of power politics proved stronger than ideological objections. If the French statesmen did not openly state that they would ally themeslves with the devil were he fighting the enemy, they acted on that theory.

Long before the Americans thought of independence French leaders calculated the effect of that event on world politics. In 1765 the French foreign minister proved his vision as a statesman, provided the key to French policy, and incidentally gave a fine illustration of how the balance-of-power system works when he wrote to his king: "England is the declared enemy of your power and your state, and she will be so always. Many ages must elapse before a durable peace can be established with this state, which looks forward to supremacy in the four quarters of the globe. Only the revolution which will occur some day in America, though we shall probably not see it, will put England back to that state of weakness in which Europe will have no more to fear of her." So French statesmen viewed the struggle between England and her colonies in terms of power politics and as an opportunity to restore the balance of power.

The Americans of 1776 did not have to read such statements to know what the policy of France would be. They knew how the balance of power must operate. And they accepted all its risks, venturing much to gain much. Perhaps the most sinister feature of power politics, in the eyes of later generations of Americans, is the formation of secret military alliances. The Americans of 1776 joyfully entered into a secret military alliance with France and owed their victory to it. True, the secret was not kept long. British intelligence had a copy of it in London in forty hours after its signature in Paris, which was rapid traveling in those days not even allowing for the time it took Dr. Bancroft, Franklin's friend and the secretary of the American Mission, to make an extra copy for the British. The military alliance, however, contained every danger a timid mind could imagine. It bound the United States to continue fighting until France, too, should lay down her arms and it guaranteed France her possessions in America for all eternity. Neither of these provisions proved harmful to the United States. It is true that France in order to get Spain into the war had to promise to continue fighting until Spain obtained Gibraltar. The United States suffered in no way and fought not an extra day. Meanwhile the military alliance paid huge dividends. France, Spain, and Holland entered the war against England, making it a general European war of power politics of which the American revolution was only one campaign. There were twice as many Frenchmen in the Yorktown campaign as there were Americans. Without the military alliance which power politics alone made possible there would almost certainly have been no American independence in 1783.

The winner at the gaming table seldom fails to return to the game. The early Americans were no exception to the rule. Time and again they entered the game of power politics and extended their winnings. Events were soon to show that they could not avoid the game no matter how hard they tried to do so.

Reference to only a few instances will illustrate the process. The United States claimed the right to the navigation of the Mississippi River, then the only outlet for people west of the Allegheny Mountains. Spain with a better right closed the river to Americans and American produce. The United States and Spain had conflicting claims to territory now in the state of Georgia. Suddenly Spain freely gave the United States all it had been claiming without power to take and without legal right. The explanation for this fortuitous gift is to be found in the power politics of Europe. Spain had been an ally of England against revolutionary France. French successes and the fear of England's growing naval power made the Spanish government decide to put an end to her war against France and accept the probable war with England. With the British navy between Spain and her possessions in America the Spanish feared the Americans would make the most of the opportunity and seize not only the items in dispute but more of the Spanish empire. To protect the greater part Spain freely gave up the Florida area in dispute and the navigation of the Mississippi. The lions contested in Europe; the jackal in America walked off with some unearned winnings.

Power politics was soon to drop a richer prize in the American lap. It has long been recognized that neither American skill in diplomacy, nor American power, nor American righteousness accounts for the Louisiana purchase. The two giants of the world, Great Britain and Napoleonic France, were locked in deadly combat, and in their struggles the vast inland empire of Louisiana was shaken loose. The United States picked it up.

The same struggle of power politics and the balance-of-power system which brought us Louisiana also brought serious dangers. That war, like all wars, tended to spread and threatened to involve the United States. The American government headed by Jefferson tried to remain aloof from power politics. It accepted humiliation, it appeased with the surrender of rights, it adopted policies which injured American prosperity, it created internal dissension that bordered on rebellion. Eventually all efforts failed and the United States entered the war. Here the dangers resulting from power politics in the world were clearly illustrated. Instead of new territorial gains from participation in power politics which the young nationalists expected, the war brought defeats, invasions, and a blockade of the coast. Yet when Britain no longer had Napoleon as an active enemy and could therefore have concentrated her strength against the partially defeated United States, the international situation came to the rescue. The chief reason the British government decided to make peace with America without exacting tangible gains was the fear of an explosion in France, just such an event as occurred when a little later Napoleon returned from Elba. The British also knew that her continental allies would support the American and not the British interpretation of maritime rights. There was already enough to quarrel about in Vienna. So the jackal which had become entangled in the fights of the lions escaped with no more serious loss than a few wounds.

An intensive study would show that power politics repeatedly and decisively affected the course of American history. The illusion of success which attended the Monroe Doctrine in its early years was the direct result of power politics. Not the American policy or the threat of American power but the inability of the competing European powers to agree on any policy, and especially the opposition of Great Britain for reasons of power politics, kept Europe from intervening in Latin

America. The balance of power in the world affected American foreign relations with the Republic of Texas, with Mexico in 1846, with Great Britain at the time of the dispute over Oregon, with Great Britain and France during the crisis of our Civil War. It was the necessities of power politics, specifically the policy of concentrating all strength in Europe to meet the threat of Germany, that induced the British to abdicate in favor of the United States the dominant position they had maintained in the Caribbean area for a century. All these episodes and many more can only be correctly understood if they are related to the international balance of power. Yet, one other episode must be mentioned because it illustrates the jackal period in our history so well. During the 1840's and '50's Great Britain, frequently joined by France, applied force to China. Successful applications compelled China to open up her ports to British and French trade, to grant extraterritoriality, and to make various other concessions. The United States played no part in the use of force. But we claimed and secured all the same concessions the others had gotten by power politics. On one occasion the American diplomats were on a steamer immediately behind the British gunboats and we shared in everything extracted from the Chinese by the use of the most-favored-nation clause in our treaties with China.

In time the United States outgrew the role of jackal. Somewhere in the '80's or '90's we assumed the proportions of a lion. The British were the first to perceive the change and to adjust their calculations accordingly. The rest of the world, and indeed most of the American people, did not note the emergence of the United States as a world power until after the Spanish-American War.

Power politics with its balance-of-power system continued to alter the course of American history, as it had previously. But in its new role the United States could not stand aloof as a frightened or hopeful spectator waiting for the decision to be reached. Now it played a direct and major part in making the decisions. It could not escape the heat of the battle nor would it leave the contest to others, since it now had power enough to determine the outcome and was not content to leave the decision to others. The possession of such power overcame even the greatest reluctance to engage in power politics. A moral philosopher might explain the process by saying one cannot avoid one's responsibilities.

At all events the United States has played the part of a lion. With undisturbed equanimity the United States has employed balance-of-power ideas and power-politics techniques in its foreign relations. It is perhaps not strange to find Theodore Roosevelt, who manifestly enjoyed the sensation of being a lion, trying to establish a balance of power in the Far East. During the course of the Russo-Japanese War he stated that "for the rest of us, while Russia's triumph would have been a blow to civilization, her destruction as an eastern Asiatic Power would also in my opinion be unfortunate. It is best that she should be left face to face with Japan so that each may have a moderative action on the other."

What is strange is to find Woodrow Wilson, who dwelt on loftier moral planes and who particularly denounced power politics, using methods worthy of the most confirmed Old World addict of the game and using them against his allies. After Germany applied to Wilson for an armistice, and before the introduction of the demanded democratic changes, Wilson consulted his allies. He proposed that the German armies should be permitted to retreat within German boundaries without any real disarmament. The Allied authorities and Wilson's own generals, Pershing and Bliss, opposed any such idea and demanded complete or crippling disarmament of the German army. Wilson instructed House to fight for his proposal and in his cable gave his reason. "It is certain," he cabled, "that too much success or security on the part of the Allies will make a genuine peace settlement difficult, if not impossible." Here is the balance-of-power technique with a vengeance. Insecurity for the Allies and insecurity guaranteed by the German army. The German army was to be too weak to stand against the combined Allied and American strength but it was to be strong enough to be a danger to the Allies without the United States. He wanted to be able to threaten, and did in fact threaten, to make a separate peace with Germany. By so doing, if the German army were still a danger to the Allies alone, he could exert enough power to make the Allies accept his terms of peace. Although Wilson lost on the armistice terms he had sufficient power to win most of the peace settlement he wanted.

These were minor episodes. The same balance-of-power policy was decisive in the major events. In seeking to understand our entry into the two world wars, our greatest and most direct participation in power politics, a major factor each time was the danger that the balance of power would be upset by a nation with a program and a philosophy hostile to ours. German submarine warfare and other violations of our rights in the first case and German conduct as well as the Japanese attack in the second instance were obviously important but no more important than our concern about the balance of power. Had there been no submarine warfare or other such events we would have entered each war on our initiative to preserve the balance of power.

Theodore Roosevelt with a flash of insight correctly predicted our course one afternoon in 1911 when the German diplomat Baron von Eckardstein called on him. "As long as England succeeds in keeping up the balance of power in Europe," said Roosevelt, "not only in principle, but in reality, well and good; should she, however, for some reason or other fail in doing so, the United States would be obliged to step in, at least temporarily, in order to re-establish the balance of power in Europe, never mind against which country or group of countries our efforts may have to be directed."

What Roosevelt predicted is what happened. When war broke out in 1914, Wilson said to Colonel House, "If Germany won it would change the course of our civilization, and make the United States a military nation." A few days later he repeated the same awareness of American involvement in world politics to the British ambassador. A year later he said to House he "had never been sure that we ought not to take part in the conflict and, if it seemed evident that Germany and her militaristic ideas were to win, the obligation upon us was greater than ever." As the war continued it was apparent that more and more Americans thought as Wilson did in terms of the balance of power and power politics.

More proof would perhaps be necessary had we not gone through the same experience again so recently. Every American adult must remember how, during 1939 and the first half of 1940, it was generally assumed in America that the war was 1914-18 over again, that the Allies would ultimately win, that their superior economic resources would tell in the end. During this period of unreality the Americans generally wanted only to stay out of the war, out of the grim business of playing the part of a major power in determining the course of events in the world. Combined with this overwhelming desire to stay aloof there was a distinct assumption of moral superiority over the wicked Europeans who indulged in power politics and brought on wars. Then came the sudden military collapse of France, and the prospect of British defeat. The balance of power was gone, and with it went the illusions of a generation of misguided thinking. Facts as obvious as Hitler in Paris and his invasion boats at the Channel are the most effective teachers in the world. The American people soon learned what the balance of power had meant to them. Even some of the pacifists realized that their pacifism had been a luxury to be enjoyed only while Great Britain, as Theodore Roosevelt had stated in 1911, had kept "the balance of power in Europe, not only in principle but in reality." Speedily policy was adjusted to the new situation and not long afterward the United States was completely involved in power politics. No thinking person who lived through that period can fail to know that most Americans understood the impossibility of remaining aloof from power politics, no matter how much we wanted to do so. The lesson was driven home to everyone when power politics reached us in the form of the Japanese attack on Pearl Harbor.

To say that the United States in one capacity or another has always been involved in power politics, that it has benefited appreciably on numerous occasions from the struggles incident to power politics, and that power politics and the balance-of-power system has meant independence and freedom for the United States as well as for others in the world, is not to say that the world should be run on any such principles. If power politics has meant those things it also means inevitable war. Conflict may often be avoided but when it comes it will, because of the balance-of-power system, involve more nations and leave devastation over a larger area. Moreover, the very process of forming competing and mutually suspicious alignments produces an atmosphere which favors the resort to war.

Whether beneficial or disastrous, power politics and the balance of power are inevitable, judging from the experience of the past centuries. There are only two other possibilities. The first would be the conquest of the world by one power which would monopolize all power and preserve peace. Rome did approximately that for several centuries. Each of you can make your own guess as to the likelihood of this solution of the problem in the near future. The second alternative is the one Wilson proposed in the League of Nations and to which the world is now vaguely committed, in theory, by the creation of the United Nations.

It is, unfortunately, necessary to stress the words "in theory" because, in fact, the United Nations as now constituted offers no solution or escape. The two decisive facts in the existing international situation are (1) all states have physical power and (2) no superior physical power exists over them. Only if these two facts are reversed can international organization eliminate power politics, the balance of power, and war. Military power must be taken away from the members of the United Nations and transferred to the United Nations. At least the relationship in terms of power must be such that the United Nations must have at its disposal overwhelming power which no nation or group of members could possibly resist. Obviously this means a surrender of sovereignty and the elimination of the veto.

The only possible hope of achieving a revolution of this character—more fundamental than what we call the American, French, or Bolshevist revolutions—is through the pending proposals on the control of atomic power. They could lead to an international authority with overwhelming power and with no veto to prevent its use. For a variety of reasons that is not likely to be accomplished although it is a bare possibility.

Meanwhile, the present United Nations is no solution. It has no power except through its members. It is not even intended to operate against any of the big powers, whose continuing unity of purpose was assumed contrary to all experience. It will not operate against any small power which is tied by interest or force to one of the big powers. Most of the small powers are already so tied and probably all will be soon. The veto of the big powers is the instrument for protecting sovereignty and is the fatal weakness.

Consequently there is no choice between power politics on one side and on the other a world system of law enforceable by the United Nations against even big powers. And consequently nations seeking to preserve their independence and to avoid rule by alien peoples will resort to politics to prevent being overpowered and will try their best to create and maintain a balance of power. If history teaches anything, it teaches that attempts will be made to destroy the balance and that war will result.

What Wilson Sent

and What House Received

Or Scholars Need to Check Carefully

PROFESSOR CHARLES SEYMOUR in *The Intimate Papers of Colonel House,* published in 1928, quoted a cable of October 29, 1918, sent by Woodrow Wilson to Colonel House in Paris as follows:

> My deliberate judgment is that our whole weight should be thrown for an armistice which will not permit a renewal of hostilities by Germany, but which will be as moderate and reasonable as possible within that condition, because lately I am certain that too much severity on the part of the Allies will make a genuine peace settlement exceedingly difficult if not impossible.... Foresight is better than immediate advantage.[1]

---

[1] *The Intimate Papers of Colonel House,* ed. Charles Seymour (4 vols.; Boston, 1926-28), IV, 110. Mr. Robert Middlekauff of the Yale University history department checked the original in the House Papers against the version printed by Seymour and says the printed version is correct except that in the final sentence the words should be, "Foresight is wiser" instead of "is better." The three dots before "Foresight" in the quotation printed by Seymour are substituted for two sentences that are so badly garbled in the manuscript as to be practically meaningless. Probably that is the reason Seymour omitted them. The exact wording was also published by Seymour in 1934 in his *American Diplomacy during the World War* (Baltimore, Md., 1934), p. 332.

In 1939, when Ray Stannard Baker published the eighth volume of *Woodrow Wilson: Life and Letters,* he wrote that on October 28, Wilson cabled House as follows:

> My deliberate judgment is that our whole weight should be thrown for an armistice which will prevent a renewal of hostilities by Germany but which will be as moderate and reasonable as possible within those limits, because it is certain that too much success or security on the part of the Allies will make a genuine peace settlement exceedingly difficult, if not impossible. The position of Haig and Milner and Petain as reported by our commander-in-chief is therefore safer than Foch's. See Baker's dispatch of today to commander-in-chief. Foresight is wiser than immediate advantage.[2]

The explanation to account for the discrepancies in language is not difficult. Seymour cites as his source the House manuscripts deposited at Yale University. His version of the cable is that which Colonel House received in Paris. Baker, using Wilson's manuscripts, states that his version of the cable was taken from a text written on the President's own typewriter. Baker did not note that there was any difference between the wording of the cable Wilson sent and the previously published wording of the message House received. No one among the scholars who have quoted the cable has apparently been aware of the conflicting language.

The cable was sent in code as Baker reports and as might be expected. According to a common practice when code is used, words are often transposed or slightly different words are used in order to protect the security of the code. In this instance it is not known whether the changes were made deliberately when encoding in America or decoding in Europe

---

[2] Ray Stannard Baker, *Woodrow Wilson: Life and Letters* (8 vols.; Garden City, N.Y., 1927-39), VIII, 523. My colleague Robert Burke requested Mr. Joseph Vance of the Manuscript Division of the Library of Congress to check the printed version given by Baker with the original manuscript in the Woodrow Wilson Papers. I am informed that the printed version reads exactly like the original.

or whether they resulted from carelessness.[3] Most of the minor variations are of no consequence: "which will prevent" is the same as "which will not permit"; "within those limits" is equivalent to "within that condition"; "because it is certain" means approximately the same as "because lately I am certain"; and "Foresight is wiser than" equals "Foresight is better than."

The other change is, however, really important. The meaning of Wilson's words "too much success or security on the part of the Allies" is significantly different from the meaning of the message House received saying "too much severity on the part of the Allies." The latter thought is on the character of the terms to be imposed on the Germans. It does not contain some of the elements in the mind of Wilson. His thinking was focused on the Allies, on their security and his desire for some insecurity so that they could be coerced by an American threat of a separate peace.

The words "too much severity" could support an interpretation of Wilson as a Lincolnian character who wished to make peace with malice toward none and with charity for all. The words "too much success or security" support the view that Wilson was not the naïve innocent which he came to be regarded but was a hard-boiled practitioner of balance-of-power politics.[4] The pictures are quite different.

[3] Mistakes were likely because of the press of business relative to the size of the clerical force. House wrote in his diary of October 30, "This morning around three o'clock, I was awakened by the motor-cycles of our messenger leaving the house with dispatches for Washington which had just been put into code. Every night since we have been here the staff has been up until three or four o'clock in the morning. The dispatches for Washington cannot be prepared and written until the evening, and the coding takes practically all night. It is necessary to get these dispatches into Washington by the early morning and the staff works at top speed during the night." *Intimate Papers*, ed. Seymour, IV, 168-169.

[4] See, for example, the way Leopold Schwarzschild uses it in *World in Trance: From Versailles to Pearl Harbor*, tr. Norbert Guterman (London, 1943), pp. 13 ff.

Both versions of the message are, of course, correct depending on the purpose for which they are to be used. If the scholar is primarily concerned with House and his negotiations with the Allies in Paris, the words he actually received are what matter. If the scholar is trying to state the policy of the United States as formulated by Wilson or to understand his mind and character, the message he composed is what counts.

Inevitably one wonders if there were other changes in thought resulting from the coding of messages between the two men and if they might have contributed to the misunderstanding that developed. At least it is clear that scholars should add alterations through coding to the long list of pitfalls they must avoid.

American Security

and Historical

and Geographical Accidents

LESS THAN a year ago an eminent American historian published an article in which he asserted that the history of the American people can only be correctly understood when interpreted in terms of the free security they enjoyed until recently.[1] He suggested the end of free security brought to a close an epoch in American history, thus challenging comparison with Frederick Jackson Turner's claim in 1893 that the disappearance of free land ended the first period of American history, a period which had lasted nearly three centuries.

That the United States alone among modern powers enjoyed national security has been so obvious that historians as well as the general public have taken it for granted, as the air which they all breathed. Indeed on the few occasions when it has been noticed, the comments were apt to express a belief that the security resulted from the superior moral virtues and wisdom of the American people.

However unnoticed or wrongly explained, the fact of se-

[1] C. Vann Woodward, "The Age of Reinterpretation," *American Historical Review,* LXVI (October, 1960), especially 1-8.

curity is incontrovertible. Professor Woodward described it in these words:

> Between the second war with England and the Second World War, the United States was blessed with a security so complete and so free that it was able virtually to do without an army and for the greater part of the period without a navy as well. Between the world war that ended in 1763 and the world wars of the twentieth century the only major military burdens placed upon the people were occasioned not by foreign threats, but by domestic quarrels, the first to establish independence for the American colonies and the second to thwart independence for the southern states. After each of these civil wars, as after all intervening wars, Americans immediately dismantled their military establishment. They followed the same procedure after each succeeding war, down to World War II, and even after that they carried demobilization to dangerous extremes before reversing the policy.

Thus the United States both had the cake of security and ate it too without paying for it. The "expensive armies and navies that took a heavy toll of the treasuries of less fortunate countries and placed severe burdens upon the backs of their people," were not known in the United States. Woodward pointed out that during the first century of the Republic's history, save in war years, annual military expenditures rarely came to as much as one per cent of the gross national product. In 1937, the proportion of military expenditures to national income was 1.5 in the United States, 5.7 in Great Britain, 9.1 in France, 23.5 in Germany and 26.4 in Russia. What this meant to the American standard of living can perhaps be appreciated by imagining what could be accomplished if the current cost of insecurity amounting to 40 odd billions of dollars were devoted to raising standards.

Certainly as important as the economic consequences was the impact of free security on the lives of American men. The demands of military service on national manpower were negligible prior to World War I as only rarely did one per cent

of the total male population between the ages of 20 and 39
see military service. "Upon the outbreak of the Civil War the
United States Army numbered a few more than sixteen thousand men, and 183 of its 198 companies were spread among
seventy-nine posts on the Indian frontier. The remaining 15
were available for 'defense' of the Canadian and Atlantic
frontiers, and the incipient Confederate frontier." When they
lost free security, the American people assumed the burden of
compulsory military service with all its costs and dangers.
Undoubtedly, Woodrow Wilson thought of such things when
he said during the period of our neutrality in World War I,
"If they [the Germans] succeed, we shall be forced to take
such measures of defense here as would be fatal to our form of
government and American ideals." So far, the dangers to our
form of government have not been realized and the only price
paid has been a portion of the lives of a large percentage of our
young men. Yet the dangers are real and are of sufficient magnitude to cause a professional soldier like Eisenhower to warn
the country of them in his farewell message as President.

Free security explains other highly significant features of
American history. I do not accept as established or even
plausible, Woodward's attribution of the Civil War to American security. His argument is as follows:

The United States is the only major country since Cromwellian
England that could afford the doubtful luxury of a full-scale civil
war of four years without incurring the evils of foreign intervention
and occupation. Had such evils been as much a foregone conclusion
as they have been among other nations, it is doubtful that Americans
would have proved as willing as they were to fall upon each other's
throats.

But I do agree fully when he traces some American mental
traits or habits to the security which came to be taken for
granted. There he finds a partial explanation of American

optimism—that sanguine temperament untroubled by anxieties about national security—of American demagogic diplomacy, of the disposition to put living standards, private indulgence, and wasteful luxury ahead of vital security requirements.

In fact, I would go further than Woodward did and would assert with confidence, although without documentary proof, that the present absence of security accounts for much in our recent behavior and for many unlovely aspects of it. After a century of assuming security as a free gift of nature, the American people have not found it easy to accept the fact of insecurity or to adjust their thoughts and lives to the new and precarious situation. They have been frustrated, baffled and nervous. It would be a great relief if there were some individual or group who could be held responsible. This makes comprehensible the excesses of the McCarthy period, the otherwise inexplicable support of even a small minority for so ridiculous a program as that of the John Birch Society, and many other things.

But, much as I agree with most of the fruitful interpretation of American history that Mr. Woodward has advanced, I am really here to disagree vigorously with his explanation of the reasons for the previous happy situation of the American people.

Free security [he wrote] was based on nature's gift of three vast bodies of water interposed between this country and any other power that might constitute a serious menace to its safety. There was not only the Atlantic to the east and the Pacific to the west, but a third body of water, considered so impenetrable as to make us virtually unaware of its importance, the Arctic Ocean and its great ice cap to the north.

I beg to differ. Of course these expanses of water played a part in America's security but it was, as I will try to demonstrate, a minor part. The true source of the free security which meant so much to the people of the United States is to be found not in the accidents of geography, but in the accidents of history.

Let me explain what I mean by historical accidents. No better example can be found than the circumstances that happened to exist during the American revolution. It was not geography to which the American rebels owed their independence. Certainly the Atlantic Ocean greatly complicated the military problem of Great Britain. No one but an idiot would deny that. Still, all the evidence supports the conclusion that troops in adequate number to put down the rebellion could have been transported and supplied across the ocean had it not been for two historical accidents. The first was the long chain of events culminating in the Whig opposition to the Government which seriously hampered its war efforts. The other, and for America, much more fortunate historical accident, was the international situation. Britain had emerged from the Seven Years War as the strongest power in the world, so strong and dominant that it was practically certain the other powers of Europe would combine against her at the first opportunity. I realize that some of you are thinking that here was no accident, that the Americans understood the possibilities of international power politics as well as the internal condition of Britain, and only started their rebellion after taking those two facts into their calculations. There is some evidence to support such a view, although I am sure that had I time, I could submit convincing evidence to the contrary. Let no one think I do not recognize the courage and ability of our early leaders. Driven by the necessities of their situation, they plunged right into the middle of the then world power politics, made an entangling and what was supposed to be a secret military alliance with a great power, recently a bitter enemy. From it all, they emerged unscathed and a winner—in fact almost the only big winner from that general world war of which the American Revolution was one campaign. All this is true, but is irrelevant here. What concerns us is American security at birth. And on this question, the facts prove beyond any doubt that the operation of the balance of power system and not the Atlantic Ocean played the decisive part in securing American independence. Once national sovereignty had been won, the problem was how to keep it. The country was relatively small in population, weak in military and industrial power, and so disunited politically that it would seem to be an easy prey for any strong aggressive nation. Somehow it managed to remain independent. Was geography or history responsible?

Let us first look to the South. Surely an accident of history, not geography, accounts for the fact that the infant United States had as its southern neighbor a weak and decaying imperial power. Suppose instead of Spain, all that vast area had been a part of Great Britain or France or even Russia. Some answer to that supposition can be found in Jefferson's policy when it appeared that France was going to replace Spain not in all the area, but only in Louisiana. As you all know, he saw such danger to American security that he tried to threaten Napoleon with the statement that the day France takes possession of New Orleans, we must marry ourselves to the British fleet and nation. This from Jefferson, the author of the slogan, "entangling alliances with none," and the leader of the pro-French or anti-British party. What better index could measure the danger he saw to American security if strong France replaced weak Spain? He saw no safety in the width of the Atlantic Ocean, nor did Napoleon see in it a decisive obstacle. It was the accident of yellow fever and the event of unexpected resistance by the Negroes of Santo Domingo that wiped out the French forces intended for Louisiana. Those facts plus others in Europe, insured the security of the United States against a powerful neighbor to the south and west.

Now let's take our security in the south a little further in history. When the prospect of intervention in Latin America by the big continental powers of Europe made it appear possible that one or more of them might obtain a foothold in that region President Monroe proclaimed that the peace and safety of the United States were at stake. We now know, especially from the monumental studies of Dexter Perkins, that what saved the United States from the apprehended danger was not the Atlantic Ocean, not the power of the United States, not even the British navy, although that historical accident was a factor, but internal conditions in Europe. In all the memoranda and statements of policy quoted by Perkins, none can be found by any European leader which cited the Atlantic Ocean as the reason for nonintervention.

The same conclusion must be reached by anyone examining the records of the French intervention in Mexico during and immediately after the Civil War. Granted that the difficulties of transporting and supplying an army across the Atlantic constituted a problem for Napoleon the Third, nowhere is that stated to be a decisive or even a serious factor in the decision of the French to withdraw. Historians have differed in their estimates of what did decide the issue, some attributing it chiefly to the presence of huge United States armies of proven quality left over from the Civil War, others finding the solution in the European international situation, in France's internal politics and in the general lack of profit in the Mexican venture. The Atlantic Ocean receives no credit.

One other aspect of security in the South requires comment. When Spanish rule over the entire area collapsed in the first quarter of the nineteenth century, how fortunate it was for the security of the United States that instead of one large unit, the Spanish Empire split into many small independent countries. Had one nation emerged extending its area from Argentina through Mexico, as the United States expanded from the Atlantic to the Pacific, the history of security in the South must surely have been different. The Rio Grande might have been fought over as often as the Rhine. The presence of a Latin America divided into many small and weak powers resulted from the process of history and in no way from the existence of the Atlantic or Pacific Oceans.

Ignoring Canada and British America for a minute, let us turn to the Arctic Ocean and its vast ice cap. That truly was a barrier to surface movement. But there is one area to the north closely connected recently with security to which a little attention can be directed. When Alaska was purchased in 1867, neither the Americans nor the Russians anticipated that its possession by either would have anything to do with American security. It is true the Russians thought American ownership might bring on an Anglo-American conflict ending in the exclusion of Britain from the Pacific Coast. It was also true that they feared they could not defend Alaska against future and probable British attacks. These considerations plus the profitlessness of the whole business and the still empty vastness of Siberia were the considerations which made Russia so eager to get out of Alaska. The importance of the purchase of Alaska for American security in recent years can scarcely be exaggerated. We should induce each American school child to contribute a penny to erect a statue to the Grand Duke Constantine who as much as any one man was responsible for Russian policy on the sale. Here, however, we are only interested in the fact that neither the Arctic Ocean nor, for that matter, the extension of the Pacific Ocean separating Alaska from Siberia were responsible for the elimination of the future insecurity Russian possession of Alaska would have been in recent years.

If the Pacific played no part in American security in the northwest corner of the continent, what of its contribution elsewhere? The first and most obvious fact to be recorded is that until the rise of Japan to the status of a great power in the twentieth century, or until Russia established a firm position on the Pacific, there was no power across the Pacific which could threaten the security of the United States. The Asiatic countries lacked military and naval power to such an extent, they were a threat to no one but themselves. Had the Pacific Ocean been no wider than Puget Sound, the United States would have been secure from attack. Later on, after Japan became a power with which to reckon, the Pacific instead of being a guarantee of security, was a source of danger to the peace of the United States. Note I said the peace and not the security of the United States, since only hysterical alarmists believed the Japanese would or could attack the continental United States. But the Philippine Islands readily accessible to the Japanese by means of the Pacific and remote across that wide ocean from America was an exposed hostage for which we might have to fight. Theodore Roosevelt, when President, regretted his ardent expansionism in the Far Pacific and said a mistake had been made.

Now let us turn again to the Atlantic and to Europe where all the great powers have been located except for the brief time Japan wielded large power and possibly except for China today. In the first decade after independence when the United States seemed an easy victim, how did we happen to escape unharmed? Did the Atlantic Ocean protect us? To me it seems clear the answer is "no." There was, first of all, the alliance with France, there was the fatigue felt by a large portion of Europe from the world war of 1756 to 1763 followed by the world war of 1778 to 1783. Then there followed the French Revolution and Napoleon with the world war or wars associated with those names. When the lions are locked in mortal combat, the small animals in the jungle enjoy a period of relative security, unless caught in the middle of the conflict. The participation of the United States in what our local history books do not call a world war, but the war of 1812, certainly raised questions of security. At first, the venture seemed reasonably safe as England had its hands fully occupied with Napoleon. But, when the latter ruled not France and most of the continent, but the tiny island of Elba, the United States did not enjoy security. Still, though the enemy now had large veteran armies to send against us, no conquest was made, no great disaster was experienced. For this, the Atlantic Ocean deserves no credit. The British saw it as an annoyance, not a barrier, and transported across it forces they hoped would be adequate. When their great General Wellington was consulted and offered the command in America, he did not mention the Atlantic as an obstacle that would prevent conquest, in fact he did not mention the Atlantic at all. He assumed there could be a conquest, but pointed out it would take a long time, would cost a lot of money, and would require command of the Great Lakes. The British government, in spite of public pressure to punish the upstart nation that had stabbed her in the back while she was fighting for the liberties of the whole world against the monster, Napoleon, had no stomach for conquest in America. They already owned plenty of empty land in Canada and elsewhere. They also had high taxes they wanted to reduce. The British Prime Minister put it bluntly in a letter to the Foreign Minister at Vienna: "The American war will not cost us less than £10,000,000 in addition to our peace establishment and other expenses. We must expect, therefore, to have it said that the property tax is continued for the purpose of securing a better frontier for Canada." Most of all, the British leaders feared a revival of Bonapartism, a fear fully justified a few months later when Napoleon returned from Elba. In all this, there was not a reference to the Atlantic as an insuperable barrier.

After Napoleon's final defeat, the United States was still

temptingly weak. Its military record in the war of 1812 was not one to strike terror in the breasts of potential enemies. Nevertheless, the United States began in 1815 the longest period of free security afforded to any large nation in modern history and perhaps in all of human history. How can this be explained? One of the first facts to be noted is that a large portion of Europe was so exhausted by the twenty-five years of heavy fighting which ended in 1815 that they were unable to embark on ambitious enterprises of overseas expansion. The two principal victors did expand; Russia across Siberia on the march to the Pacific and Great Britain in corners and areas all around the globe. The expansion of neither brought them into serious conflict with the United States as we expanded across this continent to the Pacific. In the case of Russia, there was a brief period of contact on the Pacific Coast, but on the first protests from the United States and Britain, the Russian government drew back. They had no thought of contesting possession even diplomatically. In the case of Britain, there were many points of conflicting claims and of friction—the boundary between Maine and New Brunswick, that around the Lake of the Woods and west from there to the Pacific, in the course of which Oregon became a separate area of dispute, a possible rivalry in California, the boundary of northern New York and other minor points. Fortunately for the United States, the British had no vital or important interests in these areas. There was plenty of forest and unpeopled land in Canada.

More importantly, as the result of the processes or accidents of history, the British people and government throughout most of the nineteenth century and so far in the twentieth century, subscribed to a political philosophy which in its fundamental principles approximated that of the American people and government. This similarity of attitude toward life minimized the danger of war between the two nations. Parallel philosophy and parallel interests explain the absence of insecurity on the part of the United States in the years when the British navy was so superior. Professor Woodward describes the situation in these words. "The costly navy that policed and defended the Atlantic was manned and paid for by British subjects for more than a century, while Americans enjoyed the added security afforded without cost to themselves."

This does not mean that all was serene and there were no moments of doubt. During the long months when the United States delayed the annexation of Texas because the project became entangled in party politics, the British and French governments wished to prevent this increase in American strength and sought a policy to prevent it. The reasons for their failure to translate wishes into action were the power of the United States and especially their lack of interest in the balance of power within the new world. They were willing to run risks and to pay prices for the balance of power in Europe or the world balance. This they proved a few years later in the Crimean War. But the distribution of power in North America and the prospect of the United States in the dominant position there did not appear important enough to warrant expenditure of lives or treasure.

That same explanation applies to the period of the Civil War, the centennial of which we are now inappropriately and unwisely celebrating. Vann Woodward is, I believe, strictly accurate when he wrote in the passage I have already quoted that "The United States is the only major country since Cromwellian England that could afford the doubtful luxury of a full-scale civil war of four years without incurring the evils of foreign intervention and occupation." There was, of course, a danger of intervention by Great Britain and France and not because of incidents like the Trent affair. The closest Britain came to intervention was in the late summer of 1862 when the Prime Minister and Foreign Minister agreed that the time had come to offer mediation and if the North did not accept to recognize the independence of the South. I have never understood why the North would have declared war on Britain because of such a recognition of independence. It seems to me that Lincoln was wise enough to understand he had all he could manage to fight the South alone. But wise men then, including Seward and Charles Francis Adams, and most historians since took it for granted that war would follow recognition. However that may be, the point of significance here is that the opposition to the proposed plan within the English government said nothing about the Atlantic and much about Britain's interests. The leading opponent was Sir George Cornwall Lewis. His position was that Britain had no interest at stake, there was nothing to gain so why run any risk when both sides were certain to refuse any mediation on terms the other would accept. The implication remained that if any interests were involved or anything could be gained, intervention was feasible. No doubt because of difficulties presented by the Atlantic entered into the discussion.

One more episode bearing on the role of the Atlantic and American security is worth noting. In 1895, when the United States had grown in population and industrial capacity to full stature as a major world power, there was another crisis which raised the prospect of war with Great Britain. It is not difficult to find some Americans at that time who stressed the unwisdom of a war with a nation which had a fleet so superior to ours. It is true that no American anticipated invasion by a British army and conquest. But some at least did not regard the Atlantic as a protection from the British navy. No one in Britain apparently wanted a war with the United States, yet nothing I have read suggests that their views included any thought of the Atlantic as a dominant element in the problem.

Let me repeat. I certainly do not maintain for one minute

that the existence of the Atlantic, Pacific and Arctic oceans has not been an element in the defense of the United States. I am insisting that other factors have been the dominant ones and that Vann Woodward, as well as most of the historians who have mentioned the subject, have grossly exaggerated the importance of the oceans. Let me repeat also that I fully concur in Woodward's emphasis on the need to interpret American history in the light of free security.

Ironically, the interpretation comes after the elimination of the fact. Or perhaps it is natural that historians did not see and properly evaluate the phenomenon until it had disappeared. Certainly today, we are no longer secure. Certainly also, we are paying a high price in money and in compulsory military service and perhaps in civil liberties for our insecurity. Another certainty is that planes that can fly eight thousand miles without refueling, intercontinental ballistic missiles and perhaps the nasty things space rockets can do to us, have completely destroyed whatever security was afforded by the Atlantic, Pacific and Arctic oceans.

Still, I do not want to end without calling attention to some ray of hope, however little. It seems to me that the intercontinental missiles and the space rockets, which science and technology have inflicted on us, have relieved us of the necessity of intervening directly in Cuba. Before them, the presence of a Communist regime in Cuba, or of a regime that would cooperate with the Soviet government, would surely have led to intervention. The danger of airfields for raids against us or of other operations based on Cuba would have been so great that we could not have tolerated the situation. Now that hydrogen bombs can be wafted over the North Pole, or across the Pacific, or from Europe, or perhaps dropped on us from outer space, Cuba can have no military value to Russia, and we may decide it is not necessary to intervene. If you can find any solace in that possibility, make the most of it.

Part III

The Urban Movement in American History

Some Consequences

of the Urban Movement

in American History

ABOUT TWENTY-FIVE years ago I had what I thought was an original idea. It was a new interpretation of American history which would bring understanding and give meaning to the meaningless. I remember distinctly that I had been contemplating the achievement of Frederick Jackson Turner and that I asked myself if another hypothesis could not be found to give significance to otherwise unrelated facts and to give reputation to its originator. Were there not other movements comparable to the westward movement? I do not know anything about the psychological explanations of creative thinking but with "a jar, a shock of the cerebral processes," or a flash of clarity, or what you will, I saw the answer to my inquiry.[1] There had been another movement, the urban movement. The more I thought of it the greater the significance it assumed.[2] If the westward march of the American people had

[1] Fulmer Mood uses these terms in describing Turner's achievement ("Turner's Formative Period," in *The Early Writings of Frederick Jackson Turner* [Madison, Wis., 1938], p. 5).

[2] May I at once anticipate much criticism by saying I know that the urban movement has been closely associated with the industrial revolution,

been the key to American development, as Turner said, it was
a key that worked only during the agricultural period of
American history. For the more recent period the key was
the cityward march of the American people. That and that
more than anything else could explain the transition from
the United States of Thomas Jefferson to the United States of
Franklin Roosevelt.

Alas, my pride in having conceived this tremendously important, fertile, and valid generalization was soon to be rudely
shocked. I reread Channing's fifth volume. There he has a
chapter entitled, "The Urban Migration" and it begins with
these sentences, "The westward movement forms a distinct
picture in our annals. No less distinct, but much less known,
is the rise of manufacturing and commercial cities and towns,
principally in the Northeast, and the development therein of
classes and of an industrial social system." That is all the
generalization he gives, as the balance of the chapter is devoted to the details of city life in the period 1815 to 1846, but
when I reread this passage I remembered the deep impression
it had made on me the first time I had read it and I knew
where my original idea had originated. More disturbing developments were to follow because it soon became apparent
that other students were considering the influence of the urban
movement on American history. Notable among them was
Arthur M. Schlesinger of Harvard who in 1933 published
The Rise of the City as Volume X of *A History of American
Life*. In this he tried to use the urban movement to synthesize

---

indeed in some respects the two have been so closely integrated that it is
impossible to attribute certain consequences to one or the other of these two
phenomena. The urban movement accompanied the industrial revolution
in other countries than the United States and to be correctly understood
should be studied in all its manifestations. It may also be used to cast new
light on the history of other peoples. There were, of course, cities and urban
populations and possibly urban consequences prior to the industrial revolution.

the events of American history from 1878 to 1898, when the United States "was trembling between two worlds, one rural and agricultural, the other urban and industrial."[3] His attempt was by no means completely successful but it was a remarkable pioneer effort and certainly showed he had the hypothesis in mind. A more direct expression of it appeared in an article by him in 1940 entitled "The City in American History" in which he formulated some generalizations but did not consider what I believe to be the most significant consequences of the urban movement.[4]

Of course, the fact that many Americans had been moving to the cities was a phenomenon which had long been observed by all sorts of people. Novelists were aware of it and popular writers turned from western cowboy fiction to stories of city adventure.[5] Those of us who are old enough to have read the numerous Horatio Alger books—our equivalent of the more recent "comics" and especially of Orphan Annie—will remember how often the impossibly virtuous and priggish young men went to the wicked cities to prove that virtue is rewarded. Popular songs also recorded the urban movement. One such, entitled "In the Heart of the City That Has No Heart," announced that "She wanted to roam so she left the old home" and went "to the city of no pity."[6] Statisticians mea-

---

[3] P. xiv. He was anticipating the sociologist who later wrote that "By placing the urbanization of the Western world in the center of our perspective, there is some promise that novel understandings will emerge," that the city is the center from which the influences of modern civilized life radiate to the ends of the earth, and that the problems of modern civilization are typically urban problems (Louis Wirth, "The Urban Society and Civilization," *American Journal of Sociology,* XLV [1940], 743-755).

[4] *Mississippi Valley Historical Review,* XXVII (1940), 43-66.

[5] George A. Dunlap, *The City in the American Novel, 1789-1900* (Philadelphia, 1934); John Levi Cutler, *Gilbert Patten and his Frank Merriwell Saga* (Orono, Me., 1934), p. 26.

[6] For this one I am indebted to Dr. William A. Diamond. Anyone seeking the motives of the urban migrants could well ponder the words of "How Are You Gonna Keep 'Em Down on the Farm?"

sured the growth of cities. Sociologists, more than any other group, studied the process and developed the subject of urban sociology with a large literature which historians have neglected to their cost. But few of these people, even of the sociologists, saw more than isolated facts and none used urbanization as the basis for a new synthesis. The work of the historians has so far only scratched the surface. Indeed most of their efforts have been histories of individual cities or of some small part of the urban movement. Thus Bessie Pierce's *A History of Chicago,* Bayrd Still's *Milwaukee,* or Constance McL. Green's *Holyoke, Massachusetts,* to name no others, are like the various histories of sections of the frontier such as Roosevelt's *Winning of the West* before Turner in his famous essay saw the forest as well as the trees.[7]

The failure of the historians to study the process of urbanization and its consequences is in truth curious. One would think that after several generations of writing and study of the westward movement someone would have looked for an eastward movement. Had that been done the problem of the growth of cities in the United States must have been confronted, since urbanization and the eastward movement have been intimately related.[8] That the cities have increased and since 1830 at a more rapid rate than the entire population is

[7] The most recent and best summary of the work of the historians in this field is Blake McKelvey, "American Urban History Today," *American Historical Review,* LVII (1952), 919-929.

[8] The shift of population to the cities has also resulted from a northern and northeastern movement. In this the Negroes have had a prominent but not dominant part. From 1900 to 1920 Negro urban population of the country increased by more than a million and a half while Negro rural population increased by less than 72,000. Some of the Negroes went to Southern cities, but most went to the North (T. J. Woofter, "The Negro Migration to Cities," *The Survey,* LIX [February 15, 1928], 647-649). There has also been a westward rural-urban movement, but since most of the cities in the United States, especially during the nineteenth and early twentieth centuries, have been in the East, the eastward movement has been the most important.

known and is readily established by the census reports which show that between 1790 and 1940 the total population increased 33 times while urban population increased 369 times.[9] The growth of the cities must have resulted from one, or several, of all of four processes: surplus of births over deaths, immigration from abroad, immigration from rural areas within the United States, and the expansion of city boundaries by the annexation of surrounding territory. It is impossible to determine the exact contributions of each of these to the remarkable growth that American cities have experienced. Yet it is reasonably certain that the migration from farm to city has furnished most of the large numbers involved. Fred A. Shannon has estimated that for the period between 1860 and 1900 for every urban dweller who moved to a farm there were 20 farmers who moved to a city. This conclusion leads him to suggest that Turner made a colossal mistake in describing the frontier as an avenue of escape for the oppressed city laborers and that the roles were reversed with the cities acting as a safety valve for the dissatisfied rural population.[10]

[9] This, following the recent practice of the Bureau of the Census, counts places with 2,500 or more population as urban. Schlesinger points out that between 1790 and 1890 the total population had grown 16-fold and the urban population 139-fold ("The City in American History," p. 58). His calculations used a population of 8,000 as the test for a city, as was done in the census of 1790.

[10] Fred A. Shannon, *The Farmer's Last Frontier* (New York, 1945), pp. 55, 356-359. A more detailed analysis can be found in his article "A Post Mortem on the Labor-Safety-Valve Theory," *Agricultural History*, XIX (1945), 31-37. John M. Gillette and George R. Davis in a study of the period 1900-1910 estimate that immigration contributed more than rural migration ("Measure of Rural Migration and Other Factors of Urban Increase in the United States," *American Statistical Society Publications*, XIV [1915], 642-653). A contrary estimate for the same period is given by Earle Clark ("Contributions to Urban Growth," *ibid.*, pp. 654-671). A good account can be found in the Report of the Committee on Population Problems to the National Resources Board (*The Problems of a Changing Population* [Washington, D.C., 1938], pp. 83-118). It is not possible to trace the steps by which people migrated from rural to urban America. Did they first move to small towns and then to large cities, as was done in

The facts seem to support Professor Shannon's version of the safety valve theory.

One of the important questions, the answer to which would add significantly to our understanding, if we but knew it, concerns the quality of the migrants to the cities. Have they been the most energetic, ambitious, and intelligent or have the successful and intelligent remained in agriculture while the shiftless and stupid turned from failure on the farm to possible betterment in the city? Speculation is tempting and easy. While not enough to carry conviction, the little real evidence I have found is contained in a number of studies of small samples by sociologists. For example 2,544 high school students in rural Kansas who had been given intelligence tests in 1922-1923 were studied in 1935. It was found that those who had moved to cities were those who had been measured superior in the tests of thirteen years earlier and those who had gone to the largest cities had made the highest rating. Out-of-state migrants had been superior to those who remained in Kansas.[11] Comparable studies made in various sections of the

---

Sweden, or did they jump immediately from farm to metropolis? In the census of 1940 the American people were for the first time asked where they had previously lived, in this case in 1935, so that some picture of internal migration is possible for those years. (*Sixteenth Census of the United States: 1940. Population. Internal Migration 1935 to 1940* [Washington, D.C., 1943]). See also, Warren S. Thompson, *Migration Within Ohio, 1935-40* (Oxford, Ohio, 1951); Calvin F. Schmid and Manzer John Griswold, "Migration Within the State of Washington: 1935-40," *American Sociological Review,* XVII (1952), 312-326. Dorothy Swaine Thomas, *Research Memorandum on Migration Differentials,* Social Science Research Council Bulletin 43 (1938), is an important study and contains an annotated bibliography of many of the most important sociological studies of the subject. A curious thesis bearing on urban growth can be found in Mark Jefferson, "The Law of the Primate City," *Geographical Review,* XXIX (1939), 226-232.

[11] Noel P. Gist and Carroll D. Clark, "Intelligence as a Selective Factor in Rural-Urban Migrations," *American Journal of Sociology,* XLIV (1938), 36-58; Thomas C. McCormick, "Urban Migration and Educational Selection —Arkansas Data," *ibid.,* XXXIX (1933), 355-359; Wilson Gee and Dewees

country point to the same conclusion, namely, that the urban movement has taken away the abler rural inhabitants.

Whatever the facts on this point may be, and however much the entire and neglected history of the urban movement needs to be told, I wish to bring to your attention some of its significances, some of the ways in which the urban movement explains important facts not otherwise fully understood or reveals hitherto unsuspected relationships. The first and what I believe to be the most pregnant result of the urban movement has been its effect on the birth rate. This, in turn, by a chain reaction has radically altered life in America. The crude American birth rate, i.e., the number of live births per thousand of population (and this is the best figure we can have for most of the period of United States history) was in the fifties from 1790 to 1830, in the forties until 1860, had dropped to thirty by 1900, to twenty by 1930 and then fluctuated between 16.6 and 18.9 until World War II. The dramatic reversal of this steady decline which resulted from the war is apparently a temporary phenomenon and even at its peak in 1947 the birth rate only equalled that of 1915.

The amazing drop in the birth rate by which it was cut in half between 1860 and 1930 is a revolution of the first magnitude with consequences reaching every phase of American history. It is also a direct result of urbanization. Had Theodore Roosevelt said "urban suicide" instead of "race suicide"

Runk, "Qualitative Selection in Cityward Migration," *ibid.,* XXXVII (1931), 254-265; Wilson Gee, "A Qualitative Study of Rural Development in a Single Township: 1900-1930," *ibid.,* XXXIX (1933), 210-221; W. Parker Mauln, "Selective Migration from Small Towns," *American Sociological Review,* V (1940), 748-758. For a different conclusion see Carle C. Zimmerman, "The Migration to Towns and Cities," *American Journal of Sociology,* XXXIII (1927), 105-109, and *ibid.,* pp. 237-241. Here it is stated that the cities attract the extremes, unskilled labor and professional groups, while the farms attract or retain the mean strata of society. See also Pitram Sorokin and Carle C. Zimmerman, *Principles of Rural-Urban Sociology* (New York, 1929).

he would have been describing the process accurately. It is in the cities that the greatest decline in the birth rate has regularly occurred.[12] A most thorough and convincing study based on the census of 1920 shows that the birth rate for every group—native white, foreign-born white and Negro— was lower in the cities than in the rural areas and that the larger the city the lower the birth rate.[13] The same fact is revealed by other studies at different dates. The most accurate index to population change is what is known as the net reproduction rate which has been ascertainable in the United States only during the last generation or so when reliable birth and death records have been kept. The net reproduction rate gives the number of girl babies born to 100 mothers living through the ages 15 to 50 who will also live through the ages 15 to 50. Obviously a rate of 100 would mean a stationary

[12] A. J. Jaffe, "Urbanization and Fertility," *American Journal of Sociology*, XLVIII (1942), 48-60, asserts that the differential in fertility between urban and rural areas has existed not only in Europe but among the populations of Latin American countries, among at least some of the native Asiatic populations, among the Moslems in Palestine, in Europe during the entire nineteenth century, and in Sweden as early as 1760. Dennis W. Brogan has called my attention to the fact that this statement is not true for Ireland. There the extreme poverty on the small farms so often prevented a son from marrying until his father died that the birth rate in the rural areas was lower than that in the cities.

[13] Warren S. Thompson, *Ratio of Children to Women, 1920*. Census Monograph XI (Washington, D.C., 1931). He gives the following figures on pp. 142 and 177:

Children under 5 per 1,000 Women Aged 20 to 44

	URBAN				RURAL
	Over 100,000	25,000 to 100,000	10,000 to 25,000	2,500 to 10,000	
Native white	341	390	434	477	721
Foreign-born white	679	766	861	873	998
Negro	257	294	338	370	743

population. The figure for 1940 for the entire United States was 96. This means that the American people were not reproducing themselves and that in spite of deceptive yearly increases the population was actually declining. The reason for this situation was the very low net reproduction rate of the urban portion of the population. It was only 74 compared to 114 for the rural non-farm rate and 144 for the rural farm rate.[14] In 1940, as in 1930, all the cities and in 1920 all cities above 25,000 were parasites. They could maintain their population, or grow in size, only because of the steady influx of people from the rural sections. Growth by the annexation of surrounding territory or by immigration since 1920 have been negligible factors.

The consequences of the drop in the birth rate resulting from urbanization are far-reaching and numerous. I propose to suggest only three of them to which historians have as yet given no attention.[15] The first is that the American population has grown older, or, more accurately, a steadily increasing percentage of the population is in the older age brackets.[16] America is no longer remarkable for the youthfulness of its leaders, as it was to European observers in the first part of the nineteenth century. The median age for members of the House of Representatives climbed from 41.81 in 1825 to 47.48 in 1875 and to 53.56 in 1925 and for Senators from 46.5 to 51.5 to 57.5 in the same years. Indeed, leaders of all types—judicial, diplomatic, military, naval, religious, and educational—are significantly older than their predecessors in

[14] Philip M. Hauser, "Population," *American Journal of Sociology,* XLVII (1942), 816-828.

[15] There are, of course, others which might be mentioned. For instance, one has only to compare the houses built in the 1870's when six or more children were the normal expectation with the houses built recently to appreciate the effect of the drop in the birth rate on American architecture.

[16] I do not mean that the drop in the birth rate was the sole cause of this phenomenon. Obviously the reduction in the death rate was also a factor in producing it.

the same positions.[17] If the widely held belief regarding age and conservatism is correct, both the American voters and their political leaders have been more and more inclined to conservative thinking and action. A parallel trend to older men in the leadership of the American economy may have meant that there has been less and less willingness to expand or experiment and more and more a desire to preserve the existing situation.

Conclusions on these points cannot be established by the historian's usual documentation so he generally ignores them completely. Yet surely the fact that in 1850 only 8.9 per cent of the total population were over 50 years of age and as late as 1880 only 11.8 per cent while in 1940 the figure was 20.4 per cent has implications which cannot be disregarded. Businessmen have not failed to note that the changing age composition of the population means a constantly expanding market for the goods and services older people desire. Politicians have been keenly aware of the situation. A good case could be made for the proposition that pensions for "senior citizens" have been a greater political issue during the past several decades than pensions for veterans in spite of the two world wars that produced so many veterans. The medical profession has shown its awareness of the aging population by developing a new field of specialization known as geriatrics. We who study and write history must take cognizance of this meaningful change even though we must go to unaccustomed sources for evidence.

Documentation is still more difficult in the second consequence of the reduced birth rate to which I wish to allude. This is the novel psychological experience of the Americans

---

[17] Harvey C. Lehman, "The Age of Eminent Leaders: Then and Now," *American Journal of Sociology*, LII (1947), 342-356. He gives the median and mean ages of these and many other types of leaders at various periods throughout the nineteenth century.

who grew to maturity in the period of the low birth rate. The difference between a childhood in a family where there are five or more other children and one in a family containing one or no brother or sister must be great. When the one- or two-child family became typical for so large a proportion of the population it would seem inevitable that changes in behavior and attitudes would be noticeable. Perhaps the fact that the new family pattern has produced more egocentric individuals helps to explain the high rates of divorce and of mental maladjustment which have been characteristic of urbanized America. It is not possible to speak with assurance of any of the effects of the small family on the social history of the United States since, as far as I know, no psychologist, sociologist, or historian has isolated the facts and told the story.

The facts are more easily discerned in the only other result of the drop in the birth rate to which I will refer. This is the freedom that urbanization and its birth rate have brought to American women, a freedom which has nothing to do with legal status but which is nonetheless real. In the period before the urban movement transformed life in America, woman spent her middle years, or those between 20 and 45, either pregnant or taking care of young children. The women who have gone through those years in urban America have had a vastly different experience and have known a physical and temporal freedom previously inconceivable in any human society except for a very small minority. The numerous labor-saving devices contributed by the industrial revolution, itself both a cause and an effect of the urban movement in Western civilization, merely exaggerated the freedom conferred by the small families. It is perhaps correct to say that the urban American woman has "known" rather than "enjoyed" this freedom. As a group they were caught unprepared to devote the unaccustomed leisure to activities which would yield mental, physical, or spiritual satisfaction. They have been frustrated and bored to the point of having to kill time by shopping, going to the movies, playing bridge, or in the other ways which are readily observable, and which have sometimes been seriously treated by novelists and more frequently facetiously by male cartoonists. But the historians, even those who have written social history, have yet to deal with the new phenomenon of urbanized women, though it involves directly approximately half of the American people and indirectly all the others.

The older population, the psychological patterns accompanying small families, and the altered life of American women are only some of the results of the drop in the birth rate which in turn resulted from the urban movement. Lest it be thought that the urban movement leads only down the garden path to the strange and tangled fields of psychology and sociology, let us turn to the familiar and broad highway of political history. Here the historian feels securely at home. Yet even here much will be missed and much misunderstood if not interpreted in the light of the urban movement. The most obvious facts are well known. The political opposition between urban and rural sections and the decisive part played by urban voters during the past generation have been so notorious that every radio commentator and every textbook in political science refers to them as something that every sophisticated adult knows.[18] It was in the big cities that Franklin D. Roosevelt received his huge majorities. An analysis of Roosevelt's majority of 11,000,000 in 1936 shows that with the South omitted he received 67 per cent of the votes in all cities of over 25,000 population but only 56 per cent of the rest of the votes. Nine large cities with 15 per cent of the total

[18] One of the first textbooks to show an awareness of the significance of urban politics was Arthur N. Holcombe, *The Political Parties of To-day,* published in 1924. His later textbook, *The New Party Politics,* published in 1933, placed great stress on urban politics.

population gave Roosevelt 28 per cent of his majority.[19] Since Roosevelt also carried most of the rural districts in 1936, the importance of the urban vote may have been obscured. It was to be made clearer in 1940 when Roosevelt received 60.3 per cent of the votes in all the cities of over 400,000 population and when he carried every one of them except perhaps Cincinnati, where the vote was reported with that of the rest of Hamilton County as a Willkie majority of less than 7,000. In most of the large states it was clearly the city vote which gave Roosevelt the vote of the state. Thus his majority of 230,000 in New York State resulted from his majority of 730,000 in New York City. He carried Illinois by 94,000 because he carried Chicago by 295,000. In Missouri his majority of 90,000 was possible because St. Louis and Kansas City gave him majorities of 65,000 and 30,000. In Ohio his state majority was approximately equal to his majority in Cuyahoga County in which most of the voters live in the city of Cleveland. He received the vote of Wisconsin because his majority of 73,000 votes in Milwaukee overbalanced a Willkie majority of 52,000 in the rest of the state. He failed by a narrow margin to win the vote of Michigan although Detroit gave him a majority of 173,000.[20]

The repetition of this political phenomenon has made practically everyone aware of its existence, but historians have not yet begun to seek illumination and meaning in political events by looking for a possible urban-rural conflict. Was the Progressive party of 1912 primarily an urban affair as one scholar has intimated but as none has demonstrated?[21] Was the Bryan

---

[19] David Lawrence, *Who Were the Eleven Million* (New York, 1937).

[20] Seattle *Post-Intelligencer*, November 9, 1940. In his stimulating book on *The Future of American Politics* (New York, 1952), Samuel Lubell points out (pp. 31-34) that the big city pluralities won for the Democrats in 1940, 1944, and 1948 and that the Republican hold on the largest cities as a group was broken in 1928.

[21] George E. Mowry, *Theodore Roosevelt and the Progressive Movement* (Madison, Wis., 1946), p. 280.

campaign of 1896 actually a movement of agrarian discontent as it is usually pictured? The one study of urban and rural voting in that election shows that in the states which McKinley won, Bryan had greater strength in the cities than in the rural areas, while in the states which Bryan carried his strength was rural. This, at least, proves an urban-rural tension in all sections.[22]

How necessary it is to consider urban-rural differences in politics can be appreciated by an examination of the election of 1860. As is well known, an interpretation of the Civil War has been widely accepted, especially through the writings of Charles A. Beard, which states that the controversy over slavery was largely superficial and that in essence the war was a struggle between an agricultural society and a rising industrialized or capitalistic society. There is no doubt that as one result of the war the government was dominated and its policies were fixed by the industrial, commercial, and financial groups acting through the Republican party. There is also some evidence to support the thesis that the conflict between these rival interests located in separate geographical regions brought on the war. But when the election of 1860 is analyzed by urban and rural voting some facts emerge which seriously challenge if they do not destroy this thesis. With minor exceptions, the cities of the Northeast voted against Lincoln, or if they gave him a majority it was a smaller majority than the surrounding rural area. This was true of industrial cities like Lowell and Worcester, Massachusetts, as well as of Boston or New York where commercial interests may have prevailed over industry. The rising capitalistic and industrialized society was located in these northeastern cities. Clearly the people there did not recognize Lincoln and the Republican party as their champions. It was the rural northeast that gave Lincoln

[22] William Diamond, "Urban and Rural Voting in 1896," *American Historical Review,* XLVI (1941), 281-305.

the votes of those states. Curiously a comparable situation existed in the South where the extremists had their greatest strength in the rural areas. Most of the few cities there were in the South gave majorities to the moderates, Douglas or Bell, or if to Breckinridge it was a smaller majority than the surrounding rural area gave him.[23] Some explanation other than the conflicting economic interests of agriculture and industry is required.

Indeed none of the political history of the United States since the Civil War can be considered adequate if the possible implications of an urban-rural interpretation have not been explored. National politics in America is always significantly affected and is frequently determined by its constituent elements of state politics. And in state after state the vital fact has been the continuous conflict between urban and rural voters. For years all political activity in New York State has had meaning only when interpreted in terms of New York City versus up-state. In Illinois politics has been a reflection of the antagonism between Chicago and down-state. The same situation is duplicated widely. In state after state the split between urban and rural groups is the dominant theme and in many cases the words are the same. There is scarcely a state where the urban population has not just grounds for complaining of the rotten borough system that prevails. In Ohio the census of 1940 showed that there were 698,000 people in the 22nd congressional district, most of them in the city of Cleveland, and only 163,000 in the rural 5th district. There had been no revision of congressional districts in Ohio since 1913. Some citizens of Cook County, Illinois, tried in 1946 to secure corrective action by legal means. In a suit they complained that Cook County, which meant Chicago,

[23] Ollinger Crenshaw, "Urban and Rural Voting in the Election of 1860," in Eric F. Goldman (ed.), *Historiography and Urbanization* (Baltimore, Md., 1941), pp. 43-66.

with 52 per cent of the population of the state had only nine of the twenty-five seats in Congress. The Supreme Court rejected their plea by a vote of four to three.[24] In the minority opinion, Mr. Justice Black pointed out that the complaining citizens lived in congressional election districts with populations ranging from 612,000 to 914,000, while nineteen other districts had populations under 400,000 and seven of the latter had under 200,000. The districts had been established in 1901 on the basis of the census of 1900 and there had been no redistricting in the subsequent forty years in spite of shifts in population. The local political tensions symbolized in this fashion are sometimes as important in determining who is to be elected to the Senate or to Congress as are national party labels and are often the decisive factor in deciding nominations for office within the party.

Great as is the significance of urbanization for an understanding of political activity, it is of still greater significance in accounting for the revolution in American political thought. The urban movement, more than any other development, contains the explanation of the shift from Jeffersonian democracy to the Franklin D. Roosevelt conception of democracy. Probably I should not identify the contemporary concept of democracy with Franklin D. Roosevelt for what I refer to is the very broad political philosophy to which the other Roosevelt and both Tafts also subscribed. The American people, conservatives as well as liberals, once believed that that government is best which governs least. They now believe, in varying degrees perhaps but nonetheless believe, that government should not be limited to the bare police protection of life and property but should take positive action to promote the well-being of the people. No historian, or other type of scholar, has

---

[24] Colegrove et al. v. Green et al., 328 U.S. 549. An appendix gives the congressional districts in each state with the largest and smallest populations for 1897, 1928, and 1946.

yet given an adequate account of how this revolution in political thought has occurred. It resulted, I suggest, chiefly from the fact that the American people moved to cities, in that new environment sought solutions to pressing problems and then adjusted their theory to fit the facts.[25]

The earliest instances in the expansion of urban governmental activity were concerned with the protection of health and with the fundamental utilities. Water was supplied by private companies until complaints about service or the magnitude of the problem created sufficient pressure to compel the city to take over the task. This history repeated itself in practically every large city in the United States. The persons involved did not think in the language of political philosophy. Neither did authorities of Naugatuck, Connecticut, consider the question of socialized medicine when they provided for a daily health inspection of school children and appointed a public school nurse and a dental hygienist.[26] In rural America where the farmer milked his own cow the government felt no responsibility for the sanitary conditions of milking. In urban America the protection of milk from contamination became a

[25] This does not mean that only an urbanized society will produce a government with a jurisdiction extending beyond the basic protection of life and property. Primitive societies have done so. Sumptuary laws have been known in rural societies. The mercantilist governments expanded the scope of their operations. Even in the period of Jefferson and Tom Paine there were individuals who accepted the current doctrine but urged departure from it by the government if they were to benefit. All that is meant here is that in the nineteenth and twentieth centuries, in America at least, the change in practice and thought resulted from the fact that more and more Americans lived in cities.

[26] Constance McL. Green, *History of Naugatuck, Connecticut* (New Haven, Conn., 1948), p. 157. The experience of Chicago with the problem of supplying water, which agrees in essential outline with that of every other city whose history I have read, is summarized in Bessie L. Pierce, *A History of Chicago* (New York, 1937——) II, 330-334. How urban experience changed conceptions on public education is well described in Charles Hirschfeld, *Baltimore, 1870-1900: Studies in Social History* (Baltimore, Md., 1941), chapter III.

necessity and an operation in which government exercised control over both farmer and city resident.

The same cycle of new urban problem, pressure, and expanded political authority took place again and again. In 1864 a wealthy New Yorker named Henry Bergh, who had been shocked at the sight of brutality to animals, organized a society for the prevention of cruelty to animals. He and the other members of the society did not rely on education or moral appeals but turned to government and persuaded the legislature of New York to pass a law. Then Mr. Bergh would halt overloaded street cars that some poor horse was trying to pull, would make passengers alight and even knock protesters into the gutter.[27] The movement spread to other cities where branches of the society were established and where in every case the solution of the problem was the extension of the government into a new area. In rural America each man could do with his animals what he would. When men and animals moved to the city the treatment of the animals became a problem for others and then for the government. The sphere of unrestricted freedom of individual action had been limited and the sphere of governmental activity expanded.

The solution of one problem would often be adapted to another. In 1874 a little girl was found in New York City beaten and starved by a foster mother. Since the law permitted no interference between parent and child short of mayhem or murder, she was brought as an animal to the Society for the Prevention of Cruelty to Animals. At once a society for the prevention of cruelty to children was organized and it successfully asked government to expand its activities so as to come between parent and child. In other cities similar demands led to similar action. Conceivably cruelty to children in

[27] Allan Nevins, *The Emergence of Modern America, 1865-1878* (New York, 1927), pp. 332-334.

rural areas might have produced the same results but in fact it did not.[28]

In rural America a man could spit on the ground wherever and whenever he wished. This rural habit became a public nuisance in the cities and again the scope of governmental authority was extended. The lady who led the successful agitation for an antispitting ordinance in Milwaukee urged every club woman to "carry a little silver bell to be rung at every offender, so that the man who dares to transgress will be greeted by a veritable chorus of bells at every expectoration."[29] But she and the others really depended on the power of government to correct this social and distinctively urban problem.

In rural America a man could always build any kind of a shelter or building he wished and could do with his property what he wanted, at least after Jeffersonian ideas of personal liberty supplanted the earliest mercantilist policies which tried to compel him to grow certain crops. But when more and more Americans lived in cities and when the results of unrestricted use of property became increasingly unsatisfactory a demand arose for social control. Zoning ordinances, building codes, tenement house laws, and all the other exercises of control over property by government to prevent slums or to solve urban problems represented departures from earlier standards of justifiable political action.

So it was with a host of problems which existed only when people lived in cities. None of the reformers who agitated for more government did so for principle's sake or under the influence of any political philosophy. Most of them would have denied emphatically that they wanted what we call a welfare state. All they saw was an existing evil or problem for which the obvious solution was the exercise of power by poli-

[28] *Ibid.*, pp. 334-335.
[29] Bayrd Still, *Milwaukee: The History of a City* (Madison, Wis., 1948), p. 386.

tical society. Although it is not amenable to proof by documents or statistics, surely the belief is reasonable that a half century of such action must have been a major factor in the subsequent shift in theory to an open recognition of the fact of the welfare state.

These then are some of the significances of the urban movement in American history from 1850 to 1950. Yet valid and fruitful as the thesis may be, this generalization like Turner's about the frontier can easily be misused. This hypothesis rests on the assumption that city people are alike, or at least manifest some uniformities, and are different in some respects from people living in rural areas. There is evidence to support this assumption.[30] There are also weaknesses in it. A city contains not just one but many environments as well as many groupings of people and for many human actions more meaningful conclusions can be obtained by not treating city populations as a unit. For instance, in studying elections it is profitable to look for voting by economic classes or ethnic groups within a city.[31] There are also certain powerful forces which tend to obliterate urban-rural differences. Nationalism does so. Sectionalism too may dominate over the influences tending to differentiate a city population from its rural neigh-

[30] The differences between the urban and rural birth rates and the voting records of the two groups constitute the best evidence. A prominent sociologist testing this point selected at random eighteen social characteristics on which data were available. They included such items as ratio of young to middle-aged, percentage of adults married, sex ratio of the single, death rate, amount of rent, home ownership, automobiles per capita, postal receipts, church membership, percentage of children in school. He found that in fourteen of the eighteen characteristics the cities of the North and South were more alike than the cities of either section were like the rural area of the same section (William F. Ogburn, *Social Characteristics of Cities* [Chicago, 1937], chapter VII). Too many of the social characteristics are almost inherent in the nature of cities to make this test conclusive, yet it deserves the consideration of the historian.

[31] This point is developed in an exceedingly good essay by William Diamond, "On the Dangers of an Urban Interpretation of History," in Eric F. Goldman (ed), *Historiography and Urbanization* (Baltimore, 1941).

bors. One has only to compare the attitude of both urban and rural South on FEPC proposals with those of the North to appreciate that sectionalism is to be reckoned with. A further limitation is that there is no reason to expect the urban-rural differences or tensions to remain indefinitely. Indeed the automobile, good roads, the telephone, radio, national advertising, and an amazing concatenation of other developments have been steadily urbanizing the rural areas.

Nevertheless and in spite of all qualifications, it is true, I believe, that for an understanding of American life and American history from the Civil War to the present no more fruitful interpretation exists than the significance of the urban movement.

Bibliography

1922

The Federal Board for Vocational Education: Its History, Activities and Organization (Institute for Government Research. Service Monograph of the U.S. Government, No. 6). New York: D. Appleton and Co.

The Federal Trade Commission: Its History, Activities and Organization (Institute for Government Research. Service Monograph of the U.S. Government, No. 7). New York: D. Appleton and Co.

Review of William Mitchell, *Our Air Force: The Keystone of National Defense*, in *American Historical Review*, XXVII, 599-600.

1923

The Bureau of Public Roads: Its History, Activities and Organization (Institute for Government Research. Service Monograph of the U.S. Government, No. 26). Baltimore, Md.: The Johns Hopkins Press.

The Office of the Chief of Engineers of the Army: Its Non-Military History, Activities and Organization (Institute for Government Research. Service Monograph of the U.S. Government, No. 27). Baltimore, Md.: The Johns Hopkins Press.

1924

The Federal Farm Loan Bureau: Its History, Activities and Organization (Institute for Government Research. Service Monograph of the U.S. Government, No. 34). Baltimore, Md.: The Johns Hopkins Press.

1929

The Bureau of the Census: Its History, Activities and Organization (Institute for Government Research. Service Monograph of the U.S. Government, No. 53). Washington, D.C.: The Brookings Institution.

1930

Consulting Editor, *International Bibliography of Historical Sciences.* Vol. I through XI (for the years 1926-1936). International Committee of Historical Sciences, Pierre Caron, editor. New York: H. W. Wilson, Co., 1930-1938. The American section was prepared by two scholars appointed by the American Historical Association, one of whom was Professor Holt for the years indicated.

1931

"George Washington in Later Years," in *George Washington.* Education Department, George Washington Foundation.

1933

Treaties Defeated by the Senate: A Study of the Struggle between President and Senate over the Conduct of Foreign Relations. Baltimore, Md.: The Johns Hopkins Press.

1934

Review of Claude M. Newlin, *The Life and Writings of Hugh Henry Brackenridge,* in *Modern Language Notes,* XLIX, 128-130.

1935

"John Thomas Scharf," in *Dictionary of American Biography.* New York: Scribner's, XVI, 419-420.
"The Writing of Local History in America," *Proceedings of the Middle States Association of History Teachers,* XXXIII, 76-83.

1936

"Introductory View," *Notable Narratives of the Chief Climaxes of the Victory in the World War, 1917-1919.* (*World Epochs,* Vol. X.) Washington, D.C.: United States Flag Association, pp. xi-xix.

"Charles Carroll, Barrister: The Man," *Maryland Historical Magazine,* XXXI, 112-126.

1938

Historical Scholarship in the United States, 1876-1901: As Revealed in the Correspondence of Herbert B. Adams. Baltimore, Md.: The Johns Hopkins Press.

"Henry Adams and the Johns Hopkins University," *New England Quarterly,* XI, 632-638.

1939

Review of Everett E. Edwards, *The Early Writings of Frederick Jackson Turner,* in *Journal of Southern History,* V, 387-389.

1940

"The Idea of Scientific History in America," *Journal of the History of Ideas,* I, 352-362.

Review of Gardner Waller (ed.), *Papers of John Davis Long,* in *American Historical Review,* XLV, 672-673.

1941

"The United States and the Defense of the Western Hemisphere, 1815-1940," *Pacific Historical Review,* X, 29-38.

Review of Chester P. Higby and B. T. Schantz, *John Lothrop Motley,* in *American Historical Review,* XLVII, 153-154.

1942

"The Solid South, the Birth Rate and National Politics," *Washington Alumnus,* V, 12-13.

Review of Charles Tansill, *The Foreign Policy of Thomas F. Bayard, 1885-1897,* in *Journal of Southern History,* VIII, 284-285.

Review of Leonard Hoag, *Preface to Preparedness: The Washington Disarmament Conference and Public Opinion,* in *Journal of Modern History,* XIV, 429.

1944

"John H. Latané," in *Dictionary of American Biography*. New York: Scribner's, XXI, 483-484.

1946

"The Functions of the Military Staff Committee, United Nations Organization," in *The San Francisco Conference and the United Nations Organization; Proceedings of the Institute of World Affairs, 21st Session*, XXI, No. 2, 32-37.
Review of Rayford W. Logan, *The Senate and the Versailles Mandate System*, in *Journal of Negro Education*, XV, 199-200.

1947

Review of George Mowry, *Theodore Roosevelt and the Progressive Movement*, in *Pacific Northwest Quarterly*, XXXVIII, 363-364.

1948

"Hegel, The Turner Hypothesis, and the Safety-Valve Theory," *Agricultural History*, XXII, 175-176.
Review of *Theory and Practice in Historical Study: A Report of the Committee on Historiography*, in *Pennsylvania Magazine of History and Biography*, LXXII, 80-82.
Review of Edgar E. Robinson, *They Voted for Roosevelt*, in *Pacific Historical Review*, XVII, 346-348.

1949

"An Evaluation of the Report on Theory and Practice in Historical Study," *Pacific Historical Review*, XVIII, 233-242.
"Uncle Sam as Deer, Jackal and Lion OR the United States in Power Politics," *Pacific Spectator*, III, 41-54.
Review of Ernest Samuels, *The Young Henry Adams*, in *American Historical Review*, LIV, 894-895.

1950

Review of Arthur M. Schlesinger, *Paths to the Present*, in *Mississippi Valley Historical Review*, XXXVII, 345-346.

1953

"Historical Scholarship," in *American Scholarship in the Twentieth Century*, ed. by Merle Curti. Cambridge, Mass.: Harvard University Press.

"Some Consequences of the Urban Movement in American History," *Pacific Historical Review*, XXII, 337-351.

Review of Michael Martin and Leonard Gelber, *The New Dictionary of American History*, in *American Historical Review*, LVIII, 999-1000.

1954

"Who Reads the Best Histories?" *Mississippi Valley Historical Review*, XL, 613-619.

Review of Essays and Addresses by Samuel Eliot Morison, *By Land and by Sea*, in *Mississippi Valley Historical Review*, XLI, 309-310.

1955

"History and the Social Sciences Reconsidered," *Kyklos*, Fasc. IV, pp. 389-398.

Review of Joseph P. Harris, *The Advice and Consent of the Senate: A Study of the Confirmation of Appointments by the United States Senate*, in *American Historical Review*, LX, 395-397.

Review of *The Social Sciences in Historical Study: A Report of the Committee on Historiography* (Social Science Research Council Bulletin 64, 1954), in *Pennsylvania Magazine of History and Biography*, LXXIX, 506-507.

1956

Review of Howard K. Beale (ed.), *Charles A. Beard: An Appraisal*, in *Pacific Historical Review*, XXV, 70-72.

1957

Review of Charlotte Watkins Smith, *Carl Becker: On History and the Climate of Opinion*, in *Mississippi Valley Historical Review*, XLIII, 709-710.

Review of A. S. Eisenstadt, *Charles McLean Andrews: A Study in American Historical Writing*, in *American Historical Review*, LXII, 711.

Review of Howard K. Beale, *Theodore Roosevelt and the Rise of America to World Power*, in *Political Science Quarterly*, LXXII, 436-438.

Review of Major General Courtney Whitney, *MacArthur: His Rendezvous with History*, in *World Affairs Quarterly*, XXVIII, 287-290.

1959

Review of Phil L. Snyder (ed.), *Detachment and the Writing of History: Essays and Letters of Carl L. Becker,* in *Pacific Northwest Quarterly,* L, 169-170.

1960

Reviews of Cushing Strout, *The Pragmatic Revolt in American History,* and Raymond O. Rockwood (ed.), *Carl Becker's Heavenly City Revisited,* in *American Historical Review,* LXV, 398-399.
"What Wilson Sent and What House Received: Or Scholars Need to Check Carefully," *American Historical Review,* LXV, 569-571.
Review of John Caughey, *Their Majesties the Mob,* in *Pacific Historical Review,* XXIX, 418-419.

1961

Review of Harvey Wish, *The American Historian: A Social-Intellectual History of the Writing of the American Past,* in *Mississippi Valley Historical Review,* XLVIII, 492-494.

1962

Review of David D. Van Tassel, *Recording America's Past: An Interpretation of the Development of Historical Studies in America, 1607-1884,* in *American Historical Review,* LXVII, 425-426.

1963

"The Education of Historians in the United States," *American Historical Review,* LXVIII, 402-406.
The Historical Profession in the United States (Service Center for Teachers of History, Publication No. 52). New York: Macmillan.